Civil Wars, Civil Peace

Civil Wars, Civil Peace

An Introduction to Conflict Resolution

KUMAR RUPESINGHE
with Sanam Naraghi Anderlini

Pluto Press

LONDON • STERLING, VIRGINIA

First published 1998 by Pluto Press
345 Archway Road, London N6 5AA
and 22883 Quicksilver Drive
Sterling, VA 21066-2012, USA

The rights of Kumar Rupesinghe and Sanam Naraghi Anderlini
to be identified as the authors of this work has been asserted by
them in accordance with the Copyright, Designs and Patents
Act 1988.

British Library Cataloguing in Publication Data
A catalogue record for this book is available from the
British Library

07453 12373 ✓

ISBN 0 7453 1242 X hbk

Library of Congress Cataloging in Publication Data
Rupesinghe, Kumar.
    Civil wars, civil peace: an introduction to conflict resolution/
Kumar Rupesinghe with Sanam B. Anderlini.
        p.   cm.
    ISBN 0–7453–1242–X (hardcover)
    1. Peace. 2. Diplomacy. 3. Conflict management. 4. Civil war.
I. Anderlini, Sanam M. II. Title.
JZ6045.R87   1998
327.1'7—dc21   97–44921
                                                        CIP

Designed and produced for Pluto Press by
Chase Production Services, Chadlington, OX7 3LN
Typeset by Stanford DTP Services, Northampton
Printed in the EC by Antony Rowe Ltd, Chippenham

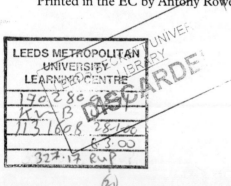

Contents

International Alert

International Alert (IA) was formed in 1985 by human rights campaigner Martin Ennals, to combat the systematic violation of rights inherent in violent conflict. The organisation was born out of a commitment to the provision and protection of social justice and human rights for all peoples, within or across borders, throughout the world. IA works to realise peace and stability within countries riven by violent conflict.

IA is a non-governmental organisation comprised of those who work for economic and social development, who protect and extend human rights and humanitarian law, and who inform, educate and persuade. IA is part of an international network of governments and nongovernmental organisations, of UN agencies, of peace, development, human rights and humanitarian movements, of academics and activists, of eminent persons and of local, national and international organisations. IA is currently active in Africa, parts of the former Soviet Union and in South Asia.

Acknowledgements

First, we would like to thank all our colleagues at International Alert from whose experience we have learnt and gained so much. Without their assistance and input, this book would not have been possible. Special thanks to Laurence Spicer for his patient reading of each draft, to Ed Garcia, Jane Sparrow, Ted Soden-Bird, Eric Abitbol, Eugenia Pisa-Lopez, Nick Killick and IA's trustees Leah Levin, Joel Joffe and Frank Judd for their comments and contributions. We would also like to thank Hayward Alker, Jürgen Dedring, Tom Woodhouse and Jan Ruysenaars for being gentle and constructive in their criticisms. We would like to express our thanks also to Elsie Arjune for her patient co-ordination of transatlantic faxes and e-mails, and to Luca Anderlini for allowing his computer to be monopolised for months on end without too many complaints. Finally, to Roger van Zwanenberg and Robert Webb of Pluto Press for their continued support and enthusiasm even as we passed our last deadline.

Foreword

Lord Judd of Portsea
Chair of International Alert

In the last decade, the nature of international relations has changed considerably. In the immediate aftermath of the collapse of Soviet power, a mood of optimism and hopeful expectation swept the world. The overarching shadow of global nuclear war had been cast off and freedom and liberty arrived in countries long used to the dark oppression of communist rule. Just as quickly, however, euphoria turned to disillusionment as this newly rediscovered independence awakened long dormant tensions in many areas of the world.

In the last decade, the ideological conflicts and the proxy wars of the cold war years have given way to disputes over identity, ethnicity and religion. And these wars are different. They are fought primarily within states not between them, the victims are predominantly civilians and they are far more resistant to outside pressure or negotiated settlements. In response to the immense and particular challenges thrown up by these new conflicts, the international community has struggled to adapt. Constructed with a view to preventing inter-state wars, the UN system has been striving to develop effective mechanisms for tackling internal conflicts. It has become increasingly clear that a fresh approach is required encompassing a greater variety of actors and exploiting innovative new tools. The burden of peace-making and peace-building is now one we must all share together, governments and citizens alike.

It is with great pleasure, then, and no little pride that I am able to introduce this book. *Civil Wars, Civil Peace* is, I believe, an important attempt to grapple with some of the most pressing concerns confronting the world today. Out of a detailed and thorough examination of the nature and characteristics of contemporary warfare, the two authors, Kumar Rupesinghe and Sanam Naraghi Anderlini, have developed a radical and original approach towards the prevention and resolution of modern internal conflicts.

In essence, the book is the culmination of Dr Rupesinghe's six years as Secretary-General of International Alert. For much of that time, it has been my privilege to work alongside him in my capacity as Chairman of the Board of Trustees where I have been fortunate enough to witness first hand his immense capacity for original and innovative thinking. It is that thinking coupled with a deep appreciation of the practical applications of his own and others' theories which emerges so forcefully in *Civil Wars, Civil Peace*. I have no hesitation, therefore, in recommending the book to all those with an interest in building a peaceful future for all peoples of the world. It is without doubt an important book and one from which we can all learn something.

Preface

Throughout my involvement in the theory and practice of conflict resolution, and specifically in outlining the difficulties associated with internal conflicts, I have witnessed a tremendous growth in the range of ideas and practical experiences in this field. Practitioners have developed new approaches in addressing the problems of conflicts and their transformation. Academics in the various social sciences are grappling with the socio-political and economic causes and solutions to conflict. Increasingly governments, intergovernmental organisations and citizen-based movements are attempting to develop new policies and strategies regarding their role in the prevention and mitigation of conflicts. In itself, this is nothing new. Successive generations, appalled by the horrors unfolding around them, have continually questioned how they might have been prevented and have sought solutions appropriate to their time. It was out of such deliberations that the United Nations was born.

For this and succeeding generations, however, war is an everyday reality, brought to us on our television screens and our radios. The resurgence of ethnicity and nationalism, culminating in the terrible carnage in Rwanda, Bosnia, Chechnya and elsewhere has stimulated renewed interest in conflict prevention and transformation. This in turn has spawned a radical change in our perceptions of conflicts and our role in them. Ordinary people are increasingly finding a voice and demanding a say in the shaping of events and the transformation of their societies. Conflict prevention is no longer the sole preserve of governments and multilateral organisations. Today, a new generation of citizen-based social movements has emerged: from large non-governmental organisations to village elders, from the corporate sector to respected individuals, the business of conflict prevention and transformation has become all-encompassing. These new institutions have taken root not only in the North, but also in the regions of conflict themselves. They have brought with them fresh approaches and developed innovative tools and instruments to help bring about conflict transformation.

In this book, our main purpose is to provide a framework and coherence with which these diverse and complex issues can be understood more easily. This book is intended to reach beyond those specifically working in this area to a wider, non-specialist audience who have an interest in contemporary international issues. In many ways, this is also a book which explains the philosophy, conceptual base and practical experiences of International Alert. Since our inception in 1985, we have worked in a number of war-torn countries, we have lobbied the international community on the need for policy coherence on conflict prevention and have provided training in conflict resolution skills to individual and partner organisations around the world. The book also draws on ideas and issues that have been raised at numerous seminars and conferences with our partners and colleagues around the world. But it is no more than an introduction to the issues and progress in this field. By virtue of being a book on *current affairs,* it cannot encompass every development. It suffers also from having been written at a time when we were heavily involved in fieldwork and so may not demonstrate the full academic rigour that the subject demands. Nevertheless, I hope that it is a useful and informative book for those interested in matters of war and peace.

Kumar Rupesinghe
February 1998

Introduction

The dynamics of fear and loathing between people of different backgrounds – ethnic or religious or economic – are not as unique or complex as we might like to believe. Violent breakdowns can occur in virtually any country during times of economic hardship, political transition or moral infirmity ... (Peter Maas, Love thy Neighbour, A Story of War)[1]

Over one million dead and up to 50 million people surviving as anonymous refugees in tents and shacks far from their homes; illiterate eight-year-olds in battle fatigues clutching AK47s, learning to kill from mercenaries paid in pockets full of precious stones; countless amputees, victims of cheap landmines covering wide tracts of land across every continent; thousands of 'rape' babies, born into a world where nobody wants them – these are the realities of war and conflict in the 1990s.

Just seven years ago the terms 'genocide' and 'ethnic cleansing' were used very selectively, mainly with reference to the Second World War, a bygone age when the evils of humanity plummeted to new depths – far removed from the civilised world of today. In 1994, the horrors of the Holocaust[2] were graphically depicted in the film *Schindler's List*. Audiences everywhere were shocked by the cruelty and inhumanity portrayed, but the majority were consoled by the belief that atrocities such as these were not taking place in their own lifetime, that human civilisation had progressed. But they were wrong. As cinema audiences recoiled from the gruesome scenes in a Hollywood movie, the Muslim population of Bosnia were reliving them. So similar was their plight, that in a letter to *The New York Times*, Louis Gentile, a diplomat working for the United Nations High Commissioner for Refugees (UNHCR) wrote:

> The terror continues, terror of attacks by armed men at night, rape and murder, children unable to sleep, huddling in fear behind boarded up doors and windows ... To those who said to themselves after seeing *Schindler's List*, 'Never again': It is happening again. The so-called leaders of the western world have known what is happening here for the last year and a half. They

receive play-by-play reports. They talk of prosecuting war criminals, but do nothing to stop the crimes.[3]

In 1994 too, in the small central African state of Rwanda, almost one million people were slaughtered during a three-month period. As the world watched these tragedies unfold on their television screens, politicians issued bland statements and the United Nations was left confused and stranded, debating the finer points of whether the term 'genocide' was applicable to the Rwandan mass killing.

Elsewhere, militia groups and state armies use conspicuous terror, rape, looting and massacre as part of their strategic military planning. The displacement of mass populations, held at the mercy of militias in refugee camps, is no longer a consequence of conflict; often it is a crucial part of the overall objective. So, as a new millennium beckons, 'genocide' and 'ethnic cleansing', and all that is associated with these terms, have not only re-entered the vocabulary, but seem to be tolerated and accepted as the *inevitable* consequences of war and conflict.

Global nuclear warfare is no longer the *primary* international security concern. It has been displaced by concerns over nuclear proliferation and excessively violent and destructive intra-state or *internal* conflicts. The realisation that the threat to one's survival may not come from long-range nuclear warheads but from sawn-off shotguns and machetes from a neighbour next door is introducing a new and more ominous dimension to our notion of human security and safety.

In 1996, an estimated 19 major internal conflicts were being fought world-wide, with a further 42 lower-intensity and 74 lethal violent political conflicts (see map[4]).

More than traditional modern warfare, internal conflicts blur the boundaries between civilians and soldiers. In Sudan over a ten-year period, 200,000 civilians died, compared with 3,000 'soldiers'. But even the term 'soldier' has different connotations since so many are children. In Liberia since the beginning of the civil war in 1989 up to the tentative peace agreement of 1996, an estimated 6,000 children were recruited as combatants. Globally an estimated 200,000–250,000 children, girls as well as boys, are fighting wars today.[5] The Gulf War television images of 'smart bombs' and sophisticated aircraft may have given an impression of minimal civilian casualties and surgical warfare, but the reality is very different. *Up to 95 per cent of war casualties are civilians.*[6] This compares to 10 per cent in the First World War and 50 per cent in the Second World War. These are innocent people trapped in conflicts of savage brutality which divide countries, towns, villages, neighbours and even families.

Why do such atrocious conflicts flare up? Why did Bosnia, Somalia and Rwanda erupt so suddenly? Were they unexpected or was conflict predicted? Why did the United Nations not take decisive action? Could anyone have prevented these tragedies? Finally, is the world faced with a future rife with violent conflicts, or will we learn how to tackle them before the next round of shots are fired? Sceptics might say that little will change and nothing can be done to stop this form of communal violence. Optimists, on the other hand, might say that not all that we see is doom and gloom, that in these same years, peaceful transitions to democracy have come about throughout Central Europe and even Latin America, and that wars in general are declining in numbers. The reality lies somewhere in between. While the violence in Bosnia, Chechnya, Guatemala and Liberia came to an end in 1996, the killings continued in Rwanda and Burundi, and in Algeria chaos raged.

The aim of this book is to attempt the daunting task of answering some of the questions raised. Our ambition is not to write the definitive text on this vast subject. Rather, our objective is to provide a simple and coherent historical, political and social framework through which we explore some of the causes of violent intra-state conflict. In doing so, we also explore the efforts being made by states, non-governmental organisations, community groups and individual citizens in their attempt to prevent, manage, resolve and ultimately *transform* situations of violent conflict into sustainable peace.

We are also attempting to bring some clarity and coherence to the terminology used to describe these complex activities. Terms such as preventive diplomacy, conflict resolution and preventive action are often used interchangeably. Yet preventive diplomacy is widely seen as the prerogative of states, while preventive action and conflict resolution refer predominantly to a range of specific activities. None encompasses the overarching conceptual aspects of the work which is being undertaken by the different actors. To resolve these and a number of other issues, we have chosen the term *conflict transformation*.[7] Our reasoning is based on a number of distinct assumptions. First, conflict *per se*, and particularly social conflict, is integral to human relations and cannot be entirely eliminated or controlled. Second, the fundamental aim of most diplomatic, preventive and resolution activities is to engage in a process through which the *violent expression* of conflict is eliminated. This can be attempted through addressing the underlying social relationships, inequities and imbalances, and providing alternative means of expression. In other words, the nature of the relationship and conflict is *transformed* from one expressed through violence and arms to one expressed through non-violent means.

High-intensity Conflicts in 1996 * (+ 1000 deaths in one year)[4]

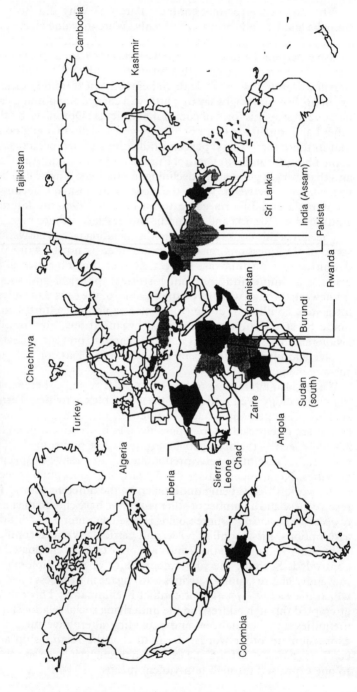

Low-intensity Conflicts

1. Guatemala
2. Mexico
3. Peru
4. Bosnia-Herz.
5. Azer/Armenia
6. Dagestan
7. Croatia
8. Angola (Cabinda)
9. Cen. Afr. Rep.
10. Ethiopia (Amhara)
11. Eth. (Oromo)
12. Eth. (Ogaden)
13. Eth. (Afar)
14. Eth. (Harar)
15. Libya
16. Mozambique (Renamo)
17. Uganda-Zaire
18. Senegal
19. Somalia
20. Somaliland
21. Uganda (LRA)
22. Ugan.WNLF
23. Ugan. (DMA)
24. S. Africa
25. Egypt
26. Iran (Kurds)
27. Iran Mujahed
28. Iraq (Kurds)
29. Iraq (shi'ites)
30. Israel
31. Lebanon
32. Bangladesh
33. India (Punjab)
34. Ind. (Manipur)
35. Ind. Nagaland
36. Ind. (Tripura)
37. Burma (Karen)
38. Bur. (Shan)
39. Bur. (Arakan)
40. China
41. Pakistan (Punjab)
42. Pak. (NWFP)

* By 1997, the Chechen conflict had ended, Liberia was entering a peaceful phase with elections, and the conflict in Zaire had abated. However in the Republic of Congo a new conflict has taken root. The official data for 1997 were not available at the time of publication.

Source: Alex Schmid and A.J. Jongman, *Mapping Violent Conflicts & Human Rights Violations in the mid-1990s* (Leiden: PIOOM, 1997)

This book is divided into five chapters. The first, introductory chapter offers a brief overview of the broad underlying geopolitical currents which are provoking internal conflict, and the United Nations' attempted response to them. Chapter 2 offers a closer examination of the predominant types of internal conflict, how they become protracted and complex, and why their resolution can seem an insurmountable task. Yet violent conflicts are rarely spontaneous. More often than not, they are the result of accumulated tensions which could have been diffused given sufficient early warning. Chapter 3 is a discussion of the ways in which early warning and early action systems could be developed to halt the escalation of violent conflicts. The limitations and obstacles that exist within current international structures are examined, and the contributions that non-state organisations and local groups could make are explored. Chapter 4 provides a historical overview of the expansion of diplomatic structures through time, and the evolution of non-state agencies and people's participation in peacemaking. We examine the concepts of 'multi-track' diplomacy, coalition-building and the diversity of tools and approaches that are needed to tackle intra-state conflicts.

Long-term peace does not come with the signing of a declaration, and the final chapter highlights factors which need to be addressed if violent conflicts are to be transformed into sustainable peace. We discuss measures which could be taken to make war impossible in the future. In doing so, we put forward the notion that there has to be a fundamental paradigm shift in the way in which violent conflicts are addressed. The prevention and resolution of modern warfare is no longer *solely* in the domain of states and inter-governmental organisations (IGOs). Although they continue to play a critical role in providing a wider and more coherent global framework for others to work within, there is a growing need for greater collaboration and co-ordination with non-state and community groups. It is time, therefore, to explore the contributions that civil society can make to building sustainable peace.

CHAPTER 1

Beyond the Cold War

The worst calamity that can befall a nation is disunity.
(Ahmad Kasravi)[1]

From World Order to Disorder

1989 and the fall of the Berlin Wall are useful starting points in attempting to come to grips with recent geopolitical changes. They not only signalled the end of a 50-year ideological battle that extended to all corners of the world, but also the end of a bipolar world where the balance of power between the Soviet Union and the United States created a semblance of world stability. When the Wall tumbled, the whole of Europe rejoiced. In Czechoslovakia, the 'Velvet Revolution' captured the world's imagination by bringing radical change through peaceful action. For a short time it seemed as if there were no other enemies or threats to *international* security and peace. Western governments were quick to capitalise on this optimism. Military budgets were cut and politicians talked about the 'peace dividend' – money that would be transferred from military expenditure to education, health and other public sectors. Meanwhile, the old Warsaw Pact countries experienced a new invasion, not of tanks and soldiers, but of businessmen anxious to reap the rewards of these new 'emerging' markets and offering a gamut of financial propositions to governments and people alike.

The euphoria did not last. As Eastern Europeans struggled to rebuild their nations, ethnic divisions and territorial conflicts that had been obscured by the Soviet Union began to resurface. Yugoslavia descended into a bleak and vicious war. Within the former Soviet Union, conflict arose between the central government and regional states such as Azerbaijan and Tajikistan, as well as between the neighbouring states themselves. In the Ukraine, a new threat emerged as the collapse of a strong central authority endangered the security of nuclear installations. In 1994, the rumblings culminated in Chechnya, where, after months of tension and antagonism, war broke out and Russian military might, reminiscent of the old Soviet days, rolled in.

In retrospect it is neither hard to understand nor difficult to sympathise with the causes of these violent outbursts. The collapse of the Soviet Union, like the collapse of any great empire, was bound to reveal faultlines hitherto concealed. It should come as no surprise to find that native Georgians, Latvians, Kazakhs or Tartars harboured resentment towards their Russian oppressors. However, lack of in-depth knowledge of the conditions within the USSR, combined with the speed at which the system collapsed, did take the world by surprise.

The collapse of communism also had wider repercussions beyond the narrow confines of East/Central Europe. Gone were the Moscow and Washington power bases which provided the arms, equipment, finance and training to sustain guerrilla groups and sympathetic governments throughout the Third World. There was no longer a need to fight over supposed strategic regions. Without superpower patronage, these groups fragmented and disintegrated. In countries such as Mozambique, the collapse of external patronage had the positive result of accelerating a peaceful end to the conflict, while elsewhere it gave birth to local potentates and modern-day warlords who turned to exploiting mineral resources such as oil, gold and diamonds for their survival. Even some state armies have been reduced to looting and pillaging from local populations to feed themselves: soldiers by day, and raiders and rebels by night. These new 'sobels' (soldier-rebels) blur the boundaries between legitimate militias, warlords and criminal gangs.

In Afghanistan, as the Soviet troops pulled out, a bloodier war for the control of political power and the lucrative narcotics trade erupted between rival factions. Regional powers – Pakistan, Iran and the newly independent ex-Soviet republics – entered the fray, competing for influence and control. The 'small wars' and conflicts that had often been created and *contained* within the wider power relations of the US and USSR were now unchecked, and the result was the spread of violence and the emergence of disparate groups, ostensibly fighting in the name of ideology, religion or ethnicity, but seeking to finance their operations through local taxation, plunder and pillage.

The Colonial Legacy

However, the end of the Cold War *alone* cannot be blamed for the breakdown of governments and the proliferation of internal conflicts. Other historic events have also played their part. But the lifting of the Iron Curtain at times serves to accentuate and even exacerbate these events. In Sri Lanka, for example, the current Tamil–Sinhalese conflict finds its roots in the post-independence years of the 1950s and a surge of Sinhalese nationalism which marginalised the Tamil population. In many African countries the difficulties faced today are rooted in the power structures devised by former colonial rulers.

The arbitrary boundaries drawn on maps in the foreign ministries of Europe divided territories and grouped long-feuding tribes under the same national identity. Many pastoral groups whose survival depended on seasonal migrations found themselves stateless and disenfranchised. The legacy of the colonial masters who passed on their authority to designated groups to rule over and impose customs on their neighbours has, over the years, developed into extreme forms of inter-tribal rivalry, and is now manifested in conflict.

In Africa particularly the struggle for independence, dominated by the mixed urban populations, concentrated on the black-white divide. Inter-tribal differences, were, in effect, overlooked as people joined forces in the fight against colonialism. But colonial systems of governance relied on a unified central structure controlling a diversity of regional tribal groups. As colonial power ebbed away, competition for central state power amongst rival tribes intensified. Democratisation and individual freedoms were never allowed to flourish so long as the power of regional native authorities and national politics was split along tribal lines. In effect strong patron–client relations, akin to traditional power structures, developed at the national level: so much so that even now, in many countries, the ethnicity of the president is indicative of the ethnic allegiances of the entire government.[2]

So long as the Cold War continued, and every scrap of land was deemed strategic, central governments, however corrupt or authoritarian, were supported and sustained by the US, the USSR or old colonial powers such as France and Great Britain. In recent years, as such support has dwindled, state economies and central governments have also weakened. In their place, regional potentates have gradually emerged. Consequently, tribalism has flourished, resulting in a splintering of centralised power bases and a greedy scramble for the control of natural resources and territory. This is reflected in countries such as Angola, the Democratic Republic of Congo (previously Zaire), Sierra Leone and Liberia, where competition over mineral resources, gold and diamond mines, logging and other lucrative businesses has descended into violence as local potentates have turned into warlords commanding their own private militias.

In countries such as Rwanda and Burundi, the social distinction between Hutu and Tutsi, largely determined by the Belgian colonials, was deliberately sustained after their departure. The minority Tutsis retained control of administrative structures and the military, relegating the majority Hutu population to a peasant existence. Hutus were thus increasingly marginalised and oppressed. As a result, within decades, ethnic distinctions which at one time had little significance, became the determining factor not just of a person's social standing, but of their very survival.

Throughout the Cold War, proxy war games, the arms race and ceaseless superpower interference did little to help the formation of stable and just societies. The maintenance of overtly corrupt and ruthless rulers like Mobuto Sese Seko in Zaire, Idi Amin in Uganda, Ferdinand and Imelda Marcos in the Philippines and a host of other military regimes and dictators across Latin America, Africa and Asia was also extremely damaging in the long run. At the time, sustaining figures such as Mobuto and Marcos was justified in the name of defending western and supposedly 'democratic' interests in the face of the communist threat. In recent years, however, the folly of pursuing such a short-sighted and self-serving policy has become all too apparent.

The Resurgence of Religion

In other parts of the world, the revival of Islam, triggered by the Iranian revolution of 1979, has caused significant shifts in the global status quo. Over the last 15 years, the Middle East, North Africa and now even Indonesia have witnessed a revival of an extreme form of Islamic fundamentalism hitherto unknown in many of these regions. In part this is a popular reaction to western cultural domination and the West's support of often corrupt regimes. It is also a reaction to the increasing disparity between the rich and poor in these areas. The clerics, who always maintained strong power bases amongst the poverty-stricken, have emerged as political figures, calling for a return to basic Koranic traditions and a rejection of any form of secularism. In Bosnia, the emergence of extremist Islamic groups is, in part, a consequence of the Muslim population's anger at what they perceived as western indifference to their plight. For the Chechens, on the other hand, the promotion of Islam as part of a new national identity is a means of distancing themselves from their former Russian rulers.

There is no doubt that Islamic ideology is being systematically manipulated by minority groups in their efforts to control entire populations. In Algeria women on city streets are deliberately terrorised and occasionally killed. In Afghanistan the Taliban, initially hailed as the saviours of the country (and supported by the US and Pakistan), have proved to be even more tyrannical than their neighbours in Iran. Even Saudi Arabia, a country notorious for its stringent Islamic law, is witnessing violent opposition in the form of extremist groups.

For Europe, with its long history of conflict with the Ottoman Empire, this rekindling of Islamic ideology is a frightening prospect. From an American perspective, the wounds are even more recent. Memories of hostage-taking in Iran and Beirut, followed by the World Trade Center bombing in New York and the bomb attack on an American base in Dharan, Saudi Arabia, add further weight to their suspicions.

In recent years, a tendency has developed, even amongst the academic community, to reminisce fondly about the certainty of the Cold War years when the enemy was a known quantity. Writers such as Samuel Huntington[3] have warned despairingly that the twenty-first century will be witness to a clash of civilisations, pitting Christian culture against Islam, Buddhism and Hinduism, amongst others. But predictions of a clash of civilisations or cultures are questionable, not least because throughout Asia, Europe and Latin America, multiculturalism has flourished for centuries. Yet the fear and suspicion are neither surprising nor entirely unjustified. None of the new Islamic governments or power bases has shown any degree of moderation or compromise either in their relations with the West, or in relation to the very people they claim to represent. Hard-line 'fundamentalists' have been deliberately outspoken in their condemnation of western culture and their desire to see it replaced by Islamic laws and values.

Care must be taken, however, not to oversimplify the issue through injudicious stereotyping. When politicians and journalists refer to parts of the Middle East as 'terrorist nations', they are, in effect, demonising entire populations. In reality stereotyping, fuelled by ignorance and the blanket use of terminology such as 'Islamic fundamentalism' not only obscures complex social and political issues in the Middle East, but potentially exacerbates them in relation to the world at large. The Islamic world is made up of a patchwork of nations, cultures, languages and histories. The danger is that by focusing on *Islam* itself, rather than on its politicisation by governments, this perceived threat could become a self-fulfilling prophecy.

The resurgence of Islam has been accompanied by a rise in other manifestations of religious extremism. While orthodox Judaism has gained in strength in the political arena in Israel, extreme forms of Christianity have also emerged. In the United States, for example, the anti-abortion lobby and right-wing Christian movements have become sufficiently strong and vocal to make an impact on the national political arena. At a time when old political ideologies and Utopias are being swept away, religion is muscling its way back on to centre stage and, in doing so, has emerged as a potent source not only of spirituality, but also of identity.

Poverty, Expectations and Structural Adjustment

Another major cause of internal conflict is poverty. Poverty *alone* does not lead to communal violence, but the awareness of *relative* poverty and expectations of a better life have always been potent ingredients in the world's richest and poorest nations. There is little doubt that despite the relative wealth of Germany in the 1930s, the ideology promulgated by the Nazis struck a chord amongst a population still reeling from the defeat of one war, and struggling against rampant inflation and unemployment.

In contrast, but with similar undertones, in Rwanda, one of the world's poorest nations, a rapidly increasing population coupled with decreasing agricultural productivity, few opportunities and uneven government support for rural areas, exacerbated social tensions. This, combined with a drop in tea and coffee prices in the late 1980s and structural adjustment policies implemented in 1990, led to even harsher living conditions and eroded the government's legitimacy in the eyes of the people. These factors in themselves did not create sufficient conditions for the outbreak of civil war or the genocide of 1994. Within the wider context, however, they were instrumental in the build-up of tension and grievance in a country with a history of social and ethnic divisions and recurrent communal violence.[4]

In recent years, despite the expansion of the middle class in India, the Far East and parts of Latin America, poverty has also increased. The world's 50 poorest nations, home to 20 per cent of the world's entire population, now account for less than 2 per cent of global income. In Latin America an estimated 200 million people live in desperate poverty, while studies suggest that in the next 30 years that figure could rise to 1.5 billion.[5] At the most basic level, an expanding population in many of the world's poorest nations is creating an ever-more acute crisis. Land scarcity and overuse have led to soil impoverishment, which in turn affects the quality and abundance of the crops. Deforestation has led to soil erosion and desertification. Natural and man-made climate change has, and will continue to have, a major impact on the quality and fertility of agricultural land, particularly in tropical regions. Dry lands and low productivity could trigger mass migrations to more fertile regions. These factors all serve to exacerbate poor living conditions and contribute to dangerous instability.

Another factor to emerge quite distinctly is the widening gap not just between rich and poor nations, but between the rich and the poor *within* nations. In 1994, the combined wealth of Mexico's 13 billionaires was more than double that of the combined wealth of the country's poorest 17 million people.[6] Personal envy alone is not a driving force for communal violence, but a claim for social justice, combined with growing intolerance of high-level corruption and increasing desperation, are undoubtedly an explosive combination.

From a global perspective, the imposition of structural adjustment programmes on the debt-ridden economies of many poor nations has too often served to make the poor even poorer. Structural adjustment policies were introduced by the World Bank's and International Monetary Fund's (IMF) assistance programmes to counter falling commodity prices and rising dollar interest rates. These policies crippled the economies of many Latin American and African states dependent on the export of raw materials. The philosophy behind these monetary and fiscal policies was that by expanding export capacities, while depressing domestic demand, the states' capacity to repay external debts would increase and the economies would gradually strengthen. Throughout the 1980s, stabilisation loans were the IMF's preferred instrument. These loans were designed to reduce local demand, devalue local currencies and control government expenditure, money supplies and rising interest rates. But their real effect was to transfer economic policies to Washington, from where pressure to deregulate local markets and liberalise economies was brought to bear.

Instead of eradicating poverty, however, too often these measures merely rubbed salt in the wounds, since little attention was given to the *distributional effects* of the policies. As the rich benefited, high-level corruption continued, leaving the poor even worse off. In Peru, a country already suffering from acute poverty and guerrilla warfare, food prices in 1990 alone jumped 2500 per cent. Unemployment soared across Africa. Even amongst those who do work, basic wages do not match their new, unsubsidised cost of living. Furthermore, state expenditure on basic utilities, health services and education was dramatically reduced. So much so that in Africa, fewer pupils will be attending primary school in the years to come.[7]

The blame cannot be shouldered by the IMF and World Bank alone, although it can be argued that by virtue of being the initiators, implementers and evaluators of these policies, these institutions are not accountable to anyone in case of failures or mistakes. In other words, they are the judge, jury and executioner of their own policies and actions. Still they are not solely responsible, and certainly the effects of structural adjustment have not been all bad. Uganda, Ghana and even Sri Lanka are amongst those nations which have, to a large extent, benefited from stringent economic policies. It should come as no surprise, however, that the implementation of such harsh policies, without a full understanding of the social and political conditions of a country, can contribute to increasing instability.

The Proliferation of Weapons and the Privatisation of Security

From Angola to Afghanistan, El Salvador and Somalia, lethal small arms, recycled Kalashnikovs and AK47s sell for less than US$

20 a piece in street markets. In a number of cities in Africa and Asia automatic weapons can even be hired on an hourly basis. The turnover of light weapons traded legally is worth an estimated US$ 5 billion, while the illegal trade is estimated to be US$ 2–10 billion.[8] What was once a state or centralised monopoly of military strength is rapidly being eroded. In its place, smaller, disparate groups, vying for economic and military control, accumulate weapons and threaten violence. In many cases where the national army no longer has the capacity to fight insurgency movements, private security firms and mercenary groups are being hired. Ex-Serbian soldiers have fought in Central Africa; South African mercenaries in Sierra Leone and Papua New Guinea. Their function has been to support national armies, to train and equip conscript soldiers, and at times to assist rebel units. The privatisation of security is a growing industry. Large multinational companies, mining operators and oil conglomerates have opted to hire professional military units to protect their installations from local guerrilla attacks.

Arms dealers may conduct their business in the offices and hotels of Bogota, Karachi, London or Moscow, but the ultimate victims of these weapons can be found across the world. From Cambodia to Bosnia, Afghanistan and across Africa, an estimated 120 million landmines continue to destroy lives and make vast tracts of land uninhabitable.[9] Trade in arms, drugs and precious stones has also proved to be profitable, and increasingly there is evidence that organised crime syndicates, diamond traders, mercenaries and a host of other groups are active in, and benefit from, internal conflicts.

The control of arms flows is a contentious issue. America, Great Britain, France, Italy, Russia and China are amongst the world's top arms-producing nations. 'Defence' is a lucrative business for these nations, and, consequently, it is immensely difficult to change government policies regarding the manufacture and sale of arms. A number of control mechanisms, including the UN's Register of Arms, already exist in relation to the sale and destination of armaments, but they are too easily bypassed. As the UK Scott Report[10] revealed, bans on the sale of arms are not adhered to in full by all governments. Additionally, the movement of small arms world-wide has become increasingly efficient and sophisticated. In many cases, arms are being recycled and sold on. For example, weapons used in the Vietnam War (1965–75) are still in circulation, having gone via Cuba to Africa. Central America is awash with weapons used by guerrilla groups and drug gangs.

In many parts of the world where internal conflict has been a feature of society for many years, the ownership of a weapon is essential for survival, both as protection and as an economic asset. Despite international efforts to demobilise guerrilla groups and decommission arms in countries where peace accords have been signed, small arms are still in circulation. So the tools of violence continue to be used against civilians. Invariably, in countries such as Angola, Guatemala and Nicaragua, where official peace has come, poverty, insecurity and fear still plague different levels of society. At a personal level, the possession of a lethal small arm alleviates some of that insecurity, but at a wider level, it encourages the spread of violence.

In addition to 'traditional' armaments, other, highly lethal weapons have become more readily available as events such as the Oklahoma bombing of 1995, the nerve gas attack on the Tokyo subway and even the chemical gas attacks of Saddam Hussein on the Kurdish villagers in Iraq and Iran throughout the 1980s have demonstrated. International conventions and bans on the use of chemical and biological weapons may exist, but they are proving inadequate in intra-state violence. Saddam Hussein's use of chemicals with such impunity has sent a disturbing message to the world: chemical and biological weapons are available and can be used.[11] The Tokyo gas attacks, and the use of cheap fertiliser to produce a bomb of such devastating effect in Oklahoma, have shown the world that technology has advanced. The blueprint for lethal weapons is no longer in the sole domain of states. Finally the spread of nuclear weapons to both state *and* non-state groups cannot be ruled out. Existing legislation cannot tackle these developments.

The Humanitarian Crisis and the Cost of War

So what is the true effect and cost of this form of violence? Josef Stalin is reputed to have commented: 'One death is a tragedy, a million is a statistic.' Apocryphal or not, it has a ring of truth to it. Everyone knows that hundreds of thousands of people were killed in Rwanda in 1994, but the exact figure is not known. Yet this is the fundamental effect of war and genocide; the destruction of lives, families and whole communities. In 1996, an estimated 50 million were living as refugees or displaced people world-wide. That is, 50 million ordinary people whose lives were devastated by war: children who will never know their real homes, elderly people who will have to learn new ways in unfamiliar countries, and men and women who find that all that remains of their life efforts is rubble, dust and memories.

There is also a crucial economic dimension to any conflict. War destroys property and agriculture. It destroys houses, schools and hospitals, industry and trade. It destroys the very infrastructure that keeps a society together. Yet little is done to prevent conflict from breaking out. As cynicism and lack of real concern dominate the political sphere of powerful nations, an enormous humanitarian industry has grown in the public sphere. It has become easier for governments to offload their share of responsibility onto relief agencies, giving an appearance of concern and generosity, whereas in reality they show little interest in addressing the root causes of these tragedies. The altruism of humanitarian and relief agencies also cloaks a great deal of self-interest. The aid business – including the agencies and their suppliers – has grown into a multi-million dollar industry. Although it is argued that such assistance is better than nothing, it is interesting and ironic to note that the food and medical aid that flow into refugee camps and war-torn areas also fuel the cycle of conflict.

At one time in Central Africa, from Rwanda to Tanzania and Zaire, *$1 million a day* was being spent on the relief camps, many harbouring the very militias guilty of committing the genocide. Over a two-year period between 1994 and 1996, militia groups such as the Rwandese Interahamwe were able to strengthen their numbers and launch attacks while living off the charitable donations of the world. Millions of dollars are spent trying to cope with these humanitarian tragedies in Africa, Asia and Europe. This is money that comes from the pockets of ordinary people wanting to help. Yet, just a fraction of that could be spent to avert such events. In 1994, as a result of the Rwandan crisis, one UK-based agency raised over US$ 87 million. Blankets, books, biscuits and boxes full of material goods were regularly collected by volunteers in Western Europe and sent to Bosnia. These humanitarian responses are commendable and necessary, but they are not enough. In peace time US$ 8 million can go a long way towards educating children, providing healthcare and creating opportunities for economic self-sufficiency. In times of war even US$ 80 million is a drop in the ocean.

It does not take an experienced politician or diplomat to realise that the prevention of violence and war is better than waiting for the death toll to rise and the refugee tides to swell. Nor does it require a great deal of expertise to appreciate the long-term troubles and difficulties that war brings to people's lives. The question, however, is what can the world at large do to help prevent the outbreak of such conflicts? Why has the so-called *international community* or United Nations seemingly failed in its task to 'eliminate the scourge of war'? As the Cold War is confined to the history books and the world stumbles into this new era of uncertainty and 'multipolarity', what global structures or international mechanisms exist or need to be created to tackle and resolve these emerging intra-state disputes?

A Step into the Past: The United Nations and the Prevention of War

The end of the Cold War did raise hopes that the UN would play a more prominent role in implementing world security and war prevention measures. Indeed for many, the massive military operation that came together under the UN banner in the 1991 Gulf War signalled President Bush's much hailed 'new world order' and an era of global security. For a short time it appeared that the Security Council, freed from the shackles of US–USSR rivalry, would finally have the power to pass and implement the numerous resolutions and conventions that had been drawn up over the years.[12]

The illusion did not last long. The oil reserves, military strength and strategic location of the Persian Gulf provided a powerful combination of reasons for the world's powers to go to war – reasons which did not exist in the case of Bosnia, Somalia or Rwanda. Besides, the Gulf War was an *inter-state* war, where one state had clearly invaded the territory of another. The United Nations had the mandate to intervene on behalf of Kuwait. But this mandate does not apply so readily to situations of internal conflict and war.

Boutros Boutros-Ghali's Agenda for Peace

The threat of internal conflicts and the UN's inability to tackle the problem were not lost on the UN's newly elected Secretary General, Boutros Boutros-Ghali in 1992. Acknowledging the increasing ethnic, religious, social and cultural tensions within state boundaries, the problems of population growth, trade barriers, debt burdens and the disparity between the rich and the poor as potential sources of regional instability, Boutros-Ghali outlined a new vision for the future of the organisation in *An Agenda for Peace*. The UN, he said, must 'stand ready to assist in peace-building in its differing contexts, rebuilding the institutions and infrastructures of *nations torn by civil war and strife* ...'.[13] Furthermore, he called for a refocusing of the UN's principal aims through the practice of *preventive diplomacy*. Preventive diplomacy referred to:

> action [taken] to prevent disputes from arising between parties, to prevent existing disputes from escalating into conflicts and to limit the spread of the latter when they occur, [requiring] measures to create confidence ... early warning based on information gathering and informal and formal fact-finding ... and may also involve preventive deployment and, in some situations, demilitarised zones.

Its objectives were:

- 'to seek to identify at the earliest possible stage, situations that could produce conflict, and to try through diplomacy to remove the sources of danger before violence results;
- where conflict erupts, to engage in peacemaking aimed at resolving the issues that have led to conflict;
- through peace-keeping, to work to preserve peace, however fragile, where fighting has been halted and to assist in implementing agreements achieved by the peacemakers;
- to stand ready to assist in peace-building in its differing contexts: rebuilding the institutions and infrastructures of nations torn by civil war and strife; and building the bonds of peaceful mutual benefit among nations formerly at war;
- and in the largest sense, to address the deepest causes of conflict; economic despair, social injustice and political oppression.'

But it quickly became clear that words were one thing, actions another. The financial crisis that plagued the UN, and a lack of support from most member states, meant that few resources were available for the implementation and development of these ideas. As a result there was little strategic planning or co-ordination within the organisation or with outside bodies. Furthermore, despite existing methods of conflict resolution, such as the use of the Secretary General's good offices in negotiation, mediation, arbitration and reconciliation, or the bolstering of the International Court of Justice, and other peacemaking instruments developed in line with Chapter IV[14] of the UN Charter, little was said about *non-military* means of conflict prevention. An expanded role for regional organisations was virtually unexplored. The contribution of non-governmental organisations and local communities and citizens in conflict prevention and resolution was no more than alluded to. The greatest emphasis was placed on the need for peacemaking through military peace enforcement.

Beyond the practical limitations of Boutros-Ghali's plans lay a number of more fundamental conceptual issues, stemming from the very nature of the United Nations as a state-based organisation. For despite Article I of the Charter, which declares that the UN should work 'to achieve *international co-operation* in solving international problems of an economic, social, cultural, or humanitarian character, and *in promoting and encouraging respect for human rights and for fundamental freedoms for all without distinction as to race, sex, language or religion*',[15] Article II (vii) states specifically that the organisation does not have the right to interfere with matters that fall into the *'domestic jurisdiction'* of any member state. So although the UN can monitor internal conflicts, abuses of human rights and the persecution of minority groups, any decision to intervene is subject to one of two conditions. First, a state must give *consent* to and *invite* intervention; and second, the Security Council needs to acknowledge that there is a wider threat to international peace and security.[16] In other words, the UN is unable or unwilling to intervene unless expressly invited into a conflict which threatens regional security. Adhering to the principle of consent means that often the UN and other intergovernmental bodies cannot intervene in the early stages of a conflict or, indeed, at any phase of the conflict cycle. In such cases as Algeria, Sri Lanka and Kashmir the UN is impotent.

Yet when it comes to internal conflict, recognition of absolute sovereignty highlights the organisation's limitations. Often it is that very sovereignty which is being questioned or opposed by movements that have no means of stating their position in a wider global arena. In the case of *international* conflicts, the UN exists as a channel for negotiations. Bilateral state diplomacy can be effective and regional intergovernmental agencies such as the Organisation of African Unity (OAU) and the Association of South-East Asian Nations (ASEAN) can participate. Within these structures, every state has official channels of communication open to the outside world. They are institutionalised and grounded in the global political arena. By contrast, such mechanisms do not exist for the resolution of internal conflicts. In other words, there are no official and legitimate channels through which insurgency movements or guerrilla groups can voice their grievances to the outside world.

The problem is compounded by the difficulty of first, identifying and, second, gaining access to opposition groups in internal conflicts. Guerrilla groups operate over a wide terrain, and often have no means of communicating with the outside world. They are able to use local populations, blend in with their environment, regularly change locations and deliberately maintain a low profile. So even establishing the first point of contact is difficult. By contrast, official representatives from countries engaged in an inter-state war are easily identifiable and readily accessible through their embassies and consulates.

Beyond that comes a longer process of trust and confidence-building. Working in isolation, insurgent movements have less chance of establishing links and building relations with the outside world. Often they are distrustful of state-based or official representatives who, by virtue of working under an explicit mandate that states any communication with insurgent groups must be with the knowledge and approval of the host government, do not appear to be impartial. This is a significant obstacle to the development of any relationships between UN representatives and non-state political groups.

Finally, in a world still dominated by *realpolitik*, the importance of *political will* cannot be underestimated. Despite the endless resolutions rubber-stamped by the UN General Assembly, it is the Security Council that retains executive powers. The Council's decision to intervene either politically or militarily in the affairs of a nation is usually based on a pressing economic or geopolitical reason. Humanitarianism alone is not a sufficient reason for spending millions of dollars or risking soldiers' lives. It is a question of power, state interests and selectivity. The truth of this was demonstrated by events in Somalia.

The UN's peace enforcement and humanitarian operation in Somalia were spearheaded by a triumphant President Bush, eager to leave his mark in the new world order. At first the world watched as US marines and soldiers headed the UN operation, landing on the beaches and making their way into the capital, Mogadishu, determined to bring relief and order to seeming chaos and anarchy. But within a short time, the same troops had become embroiled in and exacerbated a conflict that was more complex than anticipated. As the mission failed and American public interest turned to outrage, the initial humanitarian dimension was overshadowed by concern for the safety of US troops. There was no real political will or interest to explore other avenues for the resolution of the conflict. So the troops were withdrawn and the difficulties of Somalia *and the Somalians* were once again pushed aside and ignored.

The truth is that the UN is too readily seen as a stand-alone organisation, rather than the sum of all its parts. Furthermore, the wars that this organisation was created to prevent or resolve were wars that took place *between* states, not within them. The official difference between the Gulf War and Bosnia is that while in the Gulf, one state, Iraq, violated the territory of another, Kuwait, in Bosnia it was a war *within* the state. Despite the view held by some that the leaders of Serbia gave support to the Bosnian Serbs, and that the war therefore was about one state attacking another, *officially* the conflict was always treated as a civil war where *Bosnian* Muslims, Serbs and Croats were fighting each other. The same applied to Somalia and the Kurds in Iraq. With the recognition of territorial sovereignty and non-interference in domestic affairs as a bedrock of the organisation, the UN has no *immediate* mandate to send *armed* forces into any sovereign state. Without a mandate from all permanent members of the Security Council, neither the Secretariat nor the General Assembly has the authority to intervene militarily. In the case of Bosnia, this mandate was not forthcoming because of divisions within the Security Council and a general reluctance to commit troops or money.

The Cost of Failure

Never in recent times has the failure of political will had such tragic results as the Rwandan genocide of 1994. The massacres in Rwanda appeared on our television screens like scenes from a violent film, except that in Rwanda they were real. The real causes for the outbreak of genocide are complex. The reasons why it was not prevented are much simpler and directly related to the failures of political will and interest amongst the world's political leaders. Foreign observers, humanitarian workers, politicians and even the UN peacekeeping forces in Rwanda were aware of the potential for genocide for some time in advance. Yet despite the clear signals, neither the UN nor any individual government took any effective action to prevent the catastrophe. Even when the UN Secretary General made an appeal to the Security Council nothing was done. The Security Council withdrew most of the small UN observer force stationed in Rwanda and all foreign nationals, leaving the people of Rwanda at the mercy of extremists.

As the true horrors of the genocide came to light the Security Council did finally authorise a 6,800-strong peacekeeping force to be sent to Rwanda. However, a bureaucratic mix-up concerning the leasing of American armoured personnel carriers based in Germany meant that the troops had no means of transport. By the time they arrived, the slaughter had all but ended and millions had fled their homes. The world at large is not directly responsible for the genocide. That was carried out by the extremist Hutu population across the country, but the world organisation dedicated to peace did stand by and watch. So if the cost of developing new methods and structures for the prevention of conflict was deemed too high, Rwanda proved in no uncertain terms that the cost of inaction and failure was infinitely higher.

The UN's Renewed Attempts

In January 1995 Boutros-Ghali published the *Supplement to An Agenda for Peace* in which he reassessed the proposals he had set out in *An Agenda for Peace* and admitted to the difficulties in implementing those earlier recommendations. Neither the Security Council nor the Secretary General, he wrote, possesses 'the capacity to deploy, direct, command and control operations ... except perhaps on a very limited scale'.[17]

One of the major problems which the UN forces faced in Somalia in 1992, for example, was the failure of command and control. American pre-eminence in directing the military dimension of UNOSOM II (United Nations Operation in Somalia) led to confusion and a biased interpretation of the UN mandate. The decision to withdraw the UN's military mission in March 1995 even though the violence was continuing, merely reflected the Secretary General's limitations and dependence on individual governments. Instead of looking beyond military solutions, however, Boutros-Ghali's new proposal was to create a 'rapid deployment force', which would act as 'the Security Council's strategic reserve for deployment when there was an emergency need for peace-keeping troops'. The fact that many of the more powerful UN member states would be unwilling to support such a force was effectively overlooked.

In essence the UN's 'preventive diplomacy' initiative, espoused as a non-militaristic approach to peace-building, became dependent on the use of military force. Peacemaking and peace-building were interpreted as peace enforcement. The full potential of *non-military* actions was overlooked. Little importance was given to the *actual prevention* of a crisis or the development of preventive mechanisms as a *proactive* measure rather than a reaction. Furthermore, the role of regional organisations and the non-governmental sector in conflict prevention and resolution remained largely underestimated.

'We the People ... '

The UN system developed over the past 50 years has, of course, had a direct and positive impact on the populations of the UN's member states. It has created an international framework within which member states do feel a degree of responsibility and accountability towards one another. Why else should a regiment of Pakistani soldiers die in Somalia? It is because the origins of the UN system are based on the belief that our interests and our moral duty to act coincide.[18] But it is necessary to expand the system and allow for the participation of non-state groups and 'the people' in the search for peace.

In this book it is argued that non-state actors have a limited but important contribution to make in the transformation of internal conflict situations. First, given that the protagonists of violence are increasingly non-state or sub-state groups emerging from within different sectors of society, it makes sense to explore the peacemaking potentials of people from within those very same societies. Second, since in areas of internal conflict governments often face dissent from their own populace, it is critical that citizens and communities have a voice in the peace-building process. Third, it is important to recognise that diplomats, non-governmental organisations, academics, religious organisations, humanitarian fieldworkers and people directly involved in conflict areas have been constructing a vision of achieving peace through non-military and non-violent means. Making use of existing political processes, diplomatic practices, development aid, ecumenical connections and other social networks, a vision of international co-operation and co-ordination of efforts is gradually being realised. In other words 'the people' of the United Nations are increasingly more active in peace-building issues. It is important, therefore, that the UN draw on the vast potential that these groups have to offer.

Social movements have always had the capacity to make significant changes on a national and international scale. Since the early part of the twentieth century, women's movements have been successful in gaining equal opportunities and the right to vote. Human rights activists who played a pivotal role in the inclusion of human rights issues in the UN Charter have grown stronger over the decades. More recently, environmental movements have proved that even in the age of materialism and consumerism, multinational companies and governments are accountable to a wider public over problems of pollution and the destruction of the natural environment. In Europe, North America and South America there is a strong culture of civic groups focusing on single issues within a wider political agenda. These are just a few examples of movements that were started at grassroots levels in society, and have since gained enormous international momentum.

In the field of conflict resolution too, the momentum is growing as more international organisations, community-based action groups, single-issue pressure groups, academics and policy advisers take an interest in bringing peace and stability to parts of the world that the 'international community' has long ignored. Non-governmental volunteer organisations in rich countries support the work of their counterparts in poorer states. A range of non-violent conflict resolution methods are being developed for use by diverse groups in different cultural contexts. Many of the precepts are new, and may require basic changes in the general status quo of the international system. Increasingly though, there is communication and co-operation between these diverse groups, cutting across the traditional boundaries of their official, state-based counterparts. The term *multi-track diplomacy*[19] has emerged, to describe the combined and co-ordinated avenues of communication and action taken by governments, institutions, communities and individuals at international, regional, national and local levels, in an effort to bring peace and stability.

The rationale for transforming conflict situations and establishing a stable peace is not purely altruistic humanitarianism. There is little doubt that today instability and violence in any part of the world will have an impact on neighbouring countries, be they rich, stable, powerful or poor. Moreover, the economic cost of rebuilding shattered societies can be enormous. In Rwanda, the international community has already spent billions of dollars on peacekeeping operations and the provision of humanitarian aid, and that is just the beginning. In the years to come, it will have to continue to spend vast sums reconstructing the country's physical infrastructure as well as promoting reconciliation and ensuring a peaceful transformation to a stable, democratic society. Conversely, stable countries offer opportunities for development and investment. So in an interdependent world where the social and financial costs of violent upheavals are harmful to everyone, the logical and economically viable answer should surely be to focus on a means of preventing and resolving them.

Facts about Conflict[20]

- In 1996, 19 high-intensity conflicts (over 1,000 deaths p.a.) were being fought world-wide.
- In 1996, 42 low-intensity conflicts (between 100 and 1,000 deaths p.a.) and 74 lethal political conflicts were also recorded.
- Since 1945, an estimated 22 million people have died in conflicts. In 1996 alone there were over 130,000 conflict-related deaths.
- Since 1995, an estimated 37 million people have been displaced within their countries or have sought refuge elsewhere. This is an increase of 70 per cent since 1985.
- Between 200,000 and 250,000 child soldiers have fought in civil wars for government and rebel forces, some as young as five years.
- The legal and illegal sale of small arms is estimated to be worth US$ 7–15 billion p.a.
- Fifty countries produce 350 types of landmine. There are an estimated 120 million landmines planted in 64 countries. It would cost US$ 33–85 billion to clear these mines.
- Three per cent of the world's GNP is spent on the military. That amounts to US$ 700 billion p.a.
- A total of 23,597 troops were deployed in 16 UN peacekeeping and observer missions in 1996. Bangladesh, Pakistan, India, Brazil, Jordan, Poland and Canada were the major participants.
- Only six of these missions were in areas of high-intensity conflicts. The total budget for 1996 peacekeeping operations was US$ 1.5 billion, 50 per cent less than in 1995.

CHAPTER 2

Characteristics of Internal Conflicts

*War is when there is lots of shooting and they kill your family and friends
and blow big holes in the roads and houses, and you run around scared,
and you don't have enough salt to eat, and not much food either.
(Three- and four-year-old child war refugees in Mozambique,
three hours after an attack on a refugee centre)*[1]

Introduction

Living in London, New York or Tokyo, it is difficult to imagine
that even today, up to 20 wars are being fought world-wide.[2] In
the majority of cases the world at large hears little of what is
happening. Even in cases where the media focuses world attention
we rarely get a glimpse of the reality of a daily life permeated by
violence and fear. But what did it mean to live in Belfast, knowing
that on any given day a shopping expedition might turn into a lifetime
of pain?[3] How does it feel to live in Burundi, knowing that during
any night, militia men wielding guns and machetes may raid your
home and attack your family? What is it like suddenly to find your
oldest schoolfriends are hunting you down? For the people of
Bosnia and Rwanda, these fears became a reality as the violence
and conflict spread. Once violence is triggered, it seeps into society,
undermining trust and the most basic feelings of security. But why
is it triggered? What drives people to take up arms? Why do some
conflicts simmer on for years, seemingly contained and non-
threatening to the wider population, while others explode into
extensive warfare?

This chapter explores the different dimensions of violent internal
conflict. We outline the definitions and categories of armed conflict,
its general characteristics and its root causes and effects. In exploring
the increasing complexity and changing nature of contemporary
conflicts, some of the obstacles which hinder the peaceful resolution
of armed conflicts are also highlighted.

When Does a Conflict Turn into a War?

The term 'civil war' is used to describe a range of conflict situations.
Martin Van Creveld characterises a state of modern *civil* war as one

in which 'armed force is directed by social entities that are non state
... [and where] the legal monopoly of armed forces, long claimed
by the state, is wrested out of its hands, [and] existing distinctions
between war and crime ... break down'.[4] Perer Calvocoressi asserts
that civil wars are wars which 'cut across the neat and tidy
demarcations between states and non-states [and] have added to
the repertory of war'.[5]

Amongst the academic community much research is being done
on tracking and assessing conflict situations. At the forefront of this
work, the Swedish International Peace Research Institute (SIPRI)
and the Department of Peace and Conflict Research at Uppsala
University in Sweden have established a number of basic but
significant definitions or categories of conflict. One set of distinctions
is based on the scale of violence and death that results from a
conflict.[6] By and large, any conflict with over 1,000 battlefield-related
deaths per year is defined as *war* or *major armed conflict*. *Intermediate
conflicts* are those where battle-related deaths are between 25 and
1,000 during a particular year, but exceed 1,000 throughout the
duration of the conflict. Where 'violence is more sporadic and less
intense', the conflict is said to be of *low intensity*. While conflicts
in which 'one of the parties has threatened the use of violence or
has deployed military troops or made a show of force' are labelled
serious disputes.

Assessing the intensity of conflict on the basis of battlefield-related
deaths does have certain limitations, since in many cases it is
difficult to determine exactly how many deaths were a direct or
indirect consequence of a conflict. Moreover, the term battlefield
(or battle)-related implies that the victim and attacker were both
engaged in the fighting, whereas in a large number of recent cases
those killed were innocent civilians. For example, in 1995 although
the estimated deaths in Burundi were as high as 50,000, the actual
conflict was not defined as 'war', because there were few direct
military engagements. The tendency has been for the militias on
either side to attack and kill unarmed civilians. To take these
trends into account, PIOOM, a Dutch non-partisan human rights
research institute, has extended the definitions used by SIPRI and
Uppsala to base its figures on the number of *all deaths* resulting from
conflict.[7] Thus, according to PIOOM, the conflict in Burundi
during 1995 would have fallen under the '1,000 deaths or more'
category, that is, a state of war.

In the past, research in this field was limited to monitoring
conflicts in which the central government was a party to the armed
conflict. Although in a majority of internal conflicts the state is
involved, this definition does have certain shortcomings when
applied to a number of contemporary conflict situations. Somalia
was a case in point. By the time the UN troops arrived, there was

no credible government. The same could be said of Afghanistan, while in Algeria, although the government is clearly implicated in the violence, the escalation of conflict has been due to the splintering factions, which are fighting each other as much as the state.

At the University of Maryland, the Minorities at Risk Project has also developed a series of criteria for monitoring minority conflict and assessing the potential for escalation into violence and war. Recognising the rise in non-state actors and the resurgence of ethnicity as a political force, the project has been tracking and analysing the status of 270 ethno-political groups in the world's larger states. The groups monitored meet either or both of the following criteria:

> The group collectively suffers, or benefits from, systematic discriminatory treatment vis-à-vis other groups in society. The group is the basis for political mobilisation and action in defence or promotion of its self-defined interests.[8]

According to the project in 1995, 17.7 per cent of the world's population comprising 268 ethno-political groups met these criteria. The process of monitoring their conditions and analysing the scale and intensity of conflict is useful in determining where communal violence may break out. Unfortunately, given the complexity of issues being monitored, strict categorisation is not always possible and inconsistencies exist between the findings of various research institutions. Nevertheless, the results provide a distinct pattern of the trend in conflicts globally: the wars we see, and the majority of those anticipated, will be intra-state.[9]

Despite the post-Cold War proliferation of intra-state conflicts, however, there are indications that the *overall number of wars* worldwide has gradually declined in the past seven years.[10] Even in Africa, between 1989 and 1994, there was a marked decline in the number of major conflicts, from ten to six. So although the threat of violence remains acute in many areas, war itself has been at least contained. Indeed, it could be argued that the shockwaves resulting from the collapse of the Soviet Union and the ending of the Cold War have, to a large extent, settled, if only temporarily.

From Social Grievances to Armed Conflict

The existence of social or political conflict is not in itself a cause for concern. Conflict is often a source of creativity and change, and while individual people continue to relate to each other, but in pursuit of differing goals, there will always be conflicts of one kind or another. However, for the most part such conflict is not violent. Through time, social institutions have developed to allow for the resolution of civil conflicts. Police and security forces, courts of law and legislation, parliament, the press and media, and, at a lower level, even marriage councillors play an important social role, providing a structure through which grievances are voiced and conflicts are resolved peacefully. However, *when violence enters the relationship, be it between parents and children, couples, friends, neighbours or colleagues, a fundamental aspect of that relationship has disintegrated.* The same applies to relationships between different states or, more significantly, between the people of one country. The use of violence, especially organised group violence, is symbolic of a more profound breakdown in the way people relate to each other.

This violence is manifested in many ways. Johan Galtung drew attention to three different forms of social and communal violence manifested in society: direct, structural and cultural.[11]

1. *Direct violence.* This refers to armed hostile actions, when a person commits the violence, or where the violence can be traced back and attributed to a specific group. In other words, a victim can confront, name or at least point to his aggressors. In situations of outright war or under oppressive regimes, torture, executions, massacres, ethnic cleansing and rape can all be categorised as acts of direct violence. This form of violence often emerges from a more profound state of structural violence.
2. *Structural violence* refers to the endemic violence that exists in the inequalities of societal structures; in other words, where there are such gross power imbalances that people's quality of life varies substantially. Uneven resource distribution, access to medical supplies, hygiene, education, income and of course political power are a result of structural violence. Unlike a situation of direct violence, the aggressor here is intangible and faceless. It is, in effect, *the system* that bears down on every aspect of social and public life. Examples of structural violence include:

   * *The inefficient or unfair administration of justice* – which can lead to direct violence if a person or group feels unjustly treated. Currently in Rwanda, for example, an estimated 100,000 people, cramped in squalid jails, are accused of genocide. The judiciary is drastically under-resourced with few experienced prosecutors. The judicial system is flawed, corrupt and controlled by the Tutsi-dominated military. There is little hope of real justice.
   * *Sexual, religious, racial, linguistic, economic or age-based discrimination.* Apartheid South Africa was a classic example of structural violence in the form of racial discrimination. There were countless incidents of direct violence, but it was the entire system that was at fault, not just a few individuals.

- *Repression of free speech and thought* – silence comes in many forms, but in many cases it is the key to survival. In societal terms, where there is great repression, for example in Iraq or Burma, the vast majority of people dare not even think, let alone speak against the authoritarian structures that control their lives.
- *Institutional violence* is a sub-category of structural violence, but relates specifically to the violence committed by social institutions, such as the police or military forces, and which is accepted or at least tolerated by the people. For example, in the heyday of military dictatorships in Latin America it was a known fact that the police and army were responsible for the torture and murder of innocent people. But it was a fact of life and people did not have the power to challenge their authority.

3. *Cultural violence* is less easily defined, but can be identified in terms of the religious, ideological or linguistic symbols that legitimise direct or structural violence. From flags and anthems to inflammatory speeches and mythical stories, any aspect or particular elements of a culture which encourage, provoke or justify violence can be defined in terms of cultural violence. The concept of a 'chosen people' which reinforces the myth of racial or cultural supremacy can be regarded as a form of cultural violence. Examples of this include Sri Lankan Sinhalese claims of superiority over the Hindu Tamils and Nazi Germany's claims of Aryan supremacy over all other races, particularly the Jews. The myths and legends of one cultural group can be manipulated to justify the oppression and destruction of another. It is a process of dehumanising the opponent. In war, adversaries often use derogatory epithets to refer to each other. This is part of a process of dehumanising and distancing oneself from the opponent. For example, by using the term 'gook' to describe the Vietnamese during the Vietnam War, American soldiers were effectively stripping their opponents of an identity so as to make killing them seem somehow less wrong.

Guns and Survival in Southern Sudan[12]

'If I do not carry a gun, the men despise me as a defenceless woman', says a member of a local development NGO in southern Sudan. Guns are almost as well integrated into the local economy as ordinary cash may be. Guns have a market value. At one time one gun bought ten head of cattle, but with inflation, it dropped to six.

It is clear from Galtung's analysis that violence thrives on inequality in societies. In situations where political, economic, social and judicial power are concentrated in the hands of a ruling elite, the rights of a minority group may well be ignored or eroded. In such instances, it may be that armed conflict is seen as the only viable means of expressing opposition to the system, and once conflict has broken out, it becomes progressively more difficult to stop with both sides unwilling to cede ground. Over time, suspicion and mistrust create a culture of violence in which the values of a peaceful society are eroded and replaced by a different set of behavioural norms in which violence is commonplace and widely accepted.

Asymmetrical Power Relations

In internal conflicts where the state is fighting an insurgency or minority movement, the same inequality which gives expression to violence also prolongs it. These conflicts display *asymmetric* power relations.[13] Symmetric conflicts can be described as being balanced, that is, the parties involved are of equal standing. In other words, a conflict between two states such as Iran and Iraq is regarded as being symmetrical, as each government has its own military, political and diplomatic powers. The military power of one may be stronger than the other, but in terms of identity and legitimacy in the eyes of the world, there is equality. Both states have the means of waging war or proposing negotiations through political channels.

Conflicts that are asymmetrical in nature are those in which one side is more powerful or has greater international legitimacy or status than the other. This is frequently the case in internal conflicts. Often a state will use its international legitimacy and control of information to undermine insurgency groups by labelling them 'terrorists' or 'extremists'. In Indonesia, anti-government protesters are labelled 'communists'. This not only diverts attention away from their real grievances, but also serves to undermine the protest movement in the eyes of the country's own population and the world at large.

The fundamental problem with asymmetrical internal conflicts is that governments are reluctant to accept anything short of outright victory, whilst rebel groups are effectively succeeding so long as they are not crushed. The result is a stalemate in which neither side is able to make any headway. The unwillingness of governments to share their monopoly on political power and economic control is balanced by the rebels' reluctance to sacrifice their independence and the sense of identity derived from commitment to a cause. In other words, both sides fear becoming 'casualties of peace'. This is evident in Sri Lanka, the Basque Country and Northern Ireland, where strong elements within the insurgency movements are unwilling to negotiate or compromise at all.

Negotiations only become possible if there is a deadlock. This can occur when neither side sees the possibility of all-out victory, or when the cost of escalating the conflict becomes too much for either side to bear. In other words, if there is a *mutually hurting stalemate*, where *both sides are locked in a situation where they cannot escalate the conflict with their available means or at an acceptable cost.*[14] For a government this may mean facing an economic crisis, as in the case of Sri Lanka , which spent an estimated £600 million on the civil war in 1995,[15] or a public loss of faith in the government's ability to provide security and victory. Even then, the opportunity for dialogue may be slim, as both sides will try to force a change in the other's policy by taking advantage of the stalemate. In Sierra Leone, for example, the military regime was locked into a stalemate with the Revolutionary United Front Sierra Leone (RUF/SL). Throughout 1995, negotiations were delayed as the government, with external support from South African mercenaries, attempted to strengthen its position.

It is also likely that extremist elements within each party may attempt to undermine the legitimacy of the negotiators, thereby sabotaging the peace process. Hamas's suicide bombing campaign in Israel, for example, succeeded not only in undermining the legitimacy of the PLO but also that of the Israeli Labour Party, whose moderate stance was perceived as a failure by the Israeli people.

The stalemate can only be broken if there is a process of mutual recognition and willingness to partake in dialogue. Unlike inter-state conflicts which are monitored and mediated from the early stages, the escalation of internal conflict rarely elicits attempts at mediation by outside parties in the early stages. The increasing militarisation of society leads to a breakdown in communication and all socio-political and legal infrastructures that are necessary to the sustenance of civil elements of that society. In cases such as Sri Lanka or Burundi, the disputes can escalate into war and continue for years, eventually rendering most civilians indifferent to the violence that surrounds them.

A Typology of Conflict

Tracking the scale and intensity of violence is important: however, a more thorough understanding and analysis of a conflict requires identification and examination of its potential causes within a wider socio-political and economic context. As mentioned briefly in Chapter 1, since the 1980s, a series of three broad concurrent economic conditions have contributed to increasing social tensions and political conflict.[16]

1. *Stagnation and protracted decline in income.* Years of stagnant negative economic growth in poor and middle-income countries have triggered social disturbance as competition for scarce resources, jobs and other opportunities has heightened. Often in such conditions the ruling political elite can be undermined as their leadership is challenged in coups d'état. In Sierra Leone, the 24-year-old army captain, Valentine Strasser, masterminded a coup in 1991, pushing the country into deeper economic decline and eventually war. Liberia, Algeria and even the Lebanon suffered economic decline in the years preceding internal conflict.

    When the economic pie is smaller for all and power imbalances exist, often the elite or more powerful social groups prey on the weak and marginal groups in society. In the 1980s in Sudan, for example, the government targeted the marginal Dinka population, stripping them of assets, including their principal source of livelihood, cattle.[17]

2. *Unequal growth.* When there is unequal distribution amongst the population, accelerated economic growth and greater availability of material goods and resources can lead to increased tensions and, ultimately, conflict. From the Chiapas of Mexico to the majority black population of South Africa, the profound sense of injustice arose in part from a sense of relative and absolute deprivation in comparison with the ruling elite. As income disparity increases between different regions, ethnic or religious groups, or social classes, political structures are questioned and their legitimacy undermined. Pakistan is a classic example of such conditions. The ruling elite have grown richer while the majority of rural and urban populations have grown poorer. With a profoundly corrupt political system in place, recent governments have had little legitimacy in the eyes of the people, so much so that only between 25 and 30 per cent bothered to vote in the 1997 elections.

    Inequity can also be an unresolved legacy of the past. In ex-colonial states, many of the modern ruling elite are a throwback to colonial and imperial policies. They have continued having easier access to education, training and effective representation in political affairs. In contrast, the less affluent and marginalised communities continue to struggle against social imbalances and growing inequality. Often government policies offer differential treatment to particular groups, deliberately disenfranchising some. This combination of factors can result in widespread unrest and protest.

3. *Structural adjustment and changing distribution of resources.*
Throughout the 1980s and 1990s many poor states suffering
acute economic decline entered into financial stabilisation and
adjustment programmes designed by the IMF and World Bank.
Although the stringent measures imposed were necessary to tackle
macroeconomic conditions, the impact on ordinary people has
been enormous. Wages have dropped while commodity and food
prices have rocketed. Unemployment has soared and social
services such as health centres and schools have declined. Few
safety nets were in place to care for the needs of the poor. With
vast cross-sections of the public believing that such measures
favoured specific interest groups or dominant communities,
their sense of relative deprivation and injustice has at times been
manifested in protest and even violence.

In part the protracted economic decline evident in many
poor and developing countries has been a result of declining
commodity prices in the world market, a drop in aid, increased
protectionism on the part of foreign importers and unequal
distribution of assets. However, poor agricultural development
through a combination of bad government policies, slow mod-
ernisation and a range of other factors has also contributed to
declining rural productivity and increased poverty. With few
prospects, little income or hopes for a better life, many of the
young have migrated to urban areas. For most, urban life
comprises little more than unemployment and squalor, ripe
breeding grounds for mass social and political protest.

Clearly the root causes of conflicts are complex, so simple categorisation is inadequate. However, constructing loose typologies
of conflict based on the most prevalent causes helps to create a
framework in which we can examine the nature of contemporary
conflicts. These constructs are as follows:

- *resource-based conflicts* based on competition for economic
  power and access to natural resources.
- *conflicts over governance and authority* based on competition
  for political power and participation in political processes.
- *ideological conflicts* based on competition between rival ideologies
  and value systems.
- *identity conflicts* based on competition between rival ethnic,
  religious or other communal identity groups for access to
  political and economic power and social justice.

Resource-based Conflicts

Throughout its history, conflict and war over land, strategic routes,
waterways, oil, fresh water, precious minerals and a myriad of

other resources have plagued humanity. Often they come in different guises, sometimes as ethnic warfare, other times as ideological struggles, and often in circumstances of great poverty. Ironically, it is not the absolute lack of resources which breeds violence, rather it is the struggle for the *control* of certain resources which generates the worst conflicts.

An increasing global population and diminishing natural resources have also fuelled conflicts over access to agricultural land, woodlands and water. In many cases, there is a strong likelihood of conflict developing between indigenous populations and the state, as the latter attempts to exploit the natural resources in their homelands in the name of *the state*. Already in countries such as Indonesia, the government is encroaching on the life and territories of its indigenous people. Small tribes who have lived in dense forest areas throughout their history are facing the threat of extinction. The forests of islands such as Irian Jaya may be destroyed by the exploitation of copper and mineral deposits. Similar threats hang over the indigenous peoples of the Brazilian rain forests and these conflicts of interests may (and sometimes do) lead to violence. In countries as far apart as Nepal and Malawi, deforestation has resulted in soil erosion and desertification. The potential for violent conflict between an ever-increasing global population and ever-decreasing natural resources is immense.

Land Scarcity & Conflict: Contributing Factors in Rwanda[18]

Before the 1994 conflict in Rwanda 95 per cent of the population lived in rural areas and were dependent on agriculture as their prime source of income. However, intensive farming practices which strip the soil of nutrients, coupled with soil erosion, resulted in decreasing productivity. In addition, water was scarce, and the limited forests were being used for fuel-wood. Even when the government commenced a reforestation campaign, eucalyptus trees, which consume vast quantities of water and nutrients, were planted. These factors, combined with recurrent droughts in the 1980s, leading to severe water and food shortages, and made worse by a drop in world coffee prices, profoundly affected the vast majority of people.

For the Habyarimana government, whose legitimacy was based on its promise to provide for the population, failure led to a massive decline in popularity. Furthermore, it was evident that many of the government's assistance programmes were channelled into the president's home region, thus causing further resentment in the country at large. Long before the genocide was planned or violence began, peaceful protest marches and opposition parties signalled the population's desperation and concern. But little notice was taken.

As competition for land increases from Latin America to the former Soviet Union, Africa and Asia, concern for water supplies is also growing. In Malaysia, conflict exists between a traditional fishing community and the industrial sector which is polluting the sea with chemical waste. Insufficient global investment and violation of international humanitarian laws on the supply of water are factors that may lead to conflicts over water, the 'blue gold of the 21st century'.[19]

Often the problem of poor water quality is compounded by the more contentious issue of water control. This more than anything can accentuate inter-state and internal political tensions. This is particularly true in the Middle East, where Turkey's plans to build a hydroelectric dam could have a disastrous impact on Iraq. Elsewhere in the region, in the infamous Gaza Strip, control of fresh water supplies has been a source of Palestinian resentment against occupying Israeli forces.[20]

Water Supplies and Conflict: Contributing Factors in Gaza

Since 1948, when the first refugee flows started, Gaza's limited water supplies have suffered. Levels of salinity and alkalinity have risen sharply, damaging agricultural productivity. Without adequate sewerage and water quality controls, waterborne diseases are not uncommon. Since 1967, the Israeli government policies on water pricing and allocation in the region have served to intensify the crisis. By declaring all water resources to be state-owned, the government banned Arab settlers from drilling new wells or even maintaining existing ones (the prohibitions were not extended to Jewish settlers). Water allowances for Palestinians were hardly increased. In fact, citrus orchards, cisterns and natural springs were destroyed as a measure of controlling water. Declining agricultural productivity forced many Palestinians to find employment elsewhere in Israel, thus making them even more dependent on the occupiers. Even with the start of the Intifada in the late 1980s, Palestinians still had little control, as piped water supplies were regularly cut, causing widespread drought and a tremendous loss in agricultural revenue.

The pricing structures devised by the government meant that Palestinians in Gaza paid over ten times more for water than their Israeli counterparts, and four times more than residents in Israel. However, relative to their income levels, Palestinians paid up to 20 times more. So despite the government's rhetorical concern for water, it was evident that the system not only favoured Israeli settlers in Gaza, but also led to significant water wastage and over-consumption by them. In the eyes of many observers Israel 'offloaded' Gaza's impending water crisis onto Yasser Arafat and the Palestinian authorities in 1993. And although the majority of Palestinians still blame Israel for the acute problems that exist in the region, there is no doubt that the Palestinian authorities are under tremendous pressure to tackle these complex structural issues, if they are to sustain any degree of legitimacy in the eyes of the people.

Conflicts over Governance and Authority

Problems of governance invariably involve the concept of personal freedom, collective liberty and, inevitably, power. Conflicts arise over the control and distribution of political, economic, military and legislative power – all of which impact on people's freedoms. In many instances government power is used to marginalise and persecute different sectors of society. In South Africa during apartheid rule, the majority black population suffered the tyranny of a minority white population and government. Over the years, blacks were excluded from the political process, had very limited access to education, were uprooted from their homelands and families and had their daily lives controlled and monitored by the government. Challenging the authority and power of the government was an attempt to rectify the situation at its very core.

In recent years, conflicts over governance have revolved around a number of key issues.

1. State failure and decay.
2. Democracy.
3. State formation and transition.
4. Challenging secularism.

STATE FAILURE AND DECAY[21]

The common democratic assumption about the nature and role of the state is that of a coherent political and territorial entity in which a parliament provides representation and participation for citizens, and an executive branch maintains order. Yet just a glance down the list of 'states' in the world reveals how few actually qualify for this description. Totalitarian and dictatorial states have been more the norm than the exception in most parts of the developing world. Given the events of recent years, the fragmentation of the USSR, the rise in self-determination and border disputes and the general failure of some states to perform their most basic functions, the original assumption is even less applicable.

A state of decay often arises in situations where governing structures are so corrupt and controlled by despotic governments that their primary function is to exploit civil society. There is little interest on the part of the ruling elite to develop society. The objective, rather, is to exploit whatever resources are available to further their own interests. In other words, money is taken from the communal pool but never returned for collective benefit.

Often in such cases the lack of overall economic development means that there are only one or two major sources of wealth. Controlling them, therefore, confers not only financial wealth, but also military and political power. In Burma/Myanmar, the production of heroin is a major source of income for the ruling military government. In Iraq, the majority of economic activity, including the production of oil, is in the hands of a minority elite. In the former Zaire, President Mobuto Sese Seko was reputed to have all income from the gold mines diverted into his personal accounts. In each of these cases, the state structures, civil society and social services were left to decay.

However, the inability to meet the economic demands of the people and those of the international system – e.g. debt repayment – is a fundamental problem faced even by those governments who genuinely have society's best interests at heart. Not having the finances to run the country means being unable to perform even the most basic regulatory and protective tasks. Corruption becomes endemic as state employees seek to supplement their meagre incomes by demanding bribes for even the most trivial tasks. As it loses economic sovereignty, the state also loses its centrality and identity.

This gives local authorities or leaders the opportunity to galvanise support for themselves and become the focal point of economic, political and protective (or aggressive) activity. As was evident in Liberia, Chad, Sierra Leone and Somalia, the challenge to the beleaguered government comes gradually, through a process of expansion and consolidation across the country.[22] Too often it results in bloodshed and turmoil, which spiral into civil war.

DEMOCRACY

A struggle for democracy is in essence a shift in power relations. But given that the ruling elite are often reluctant to share their power, the likelihood of conflict developing can be high. Burma's ruling junta offers a particularly apt example of this reluctance. Elections were held and the democratic party of Aung San Suu Kyi won an overwhelming victory. But instead of stepping down, the military rulers hung on to power, persecuting and killing protesters and dissidents. In other countries there may be no alternatives to the existing state and government, so those in power have the means to label themselves democratic, whereas in reality they are heading one-party states. In Iran, for example, elections are held (indeed, the electorate risks punitive action if they do not vote), but candidates are vetted, freedom of speech is severely curtailed and political dissidence is not tolerated. Even in the 1997 presidential elections which swept the 'liberal' Mohammed Khattami to victory, candidates were carefully selected by the Council of Guardians. From an estimated 250 prospective candidates for the post, the Council accepted just four; all of whom were clerics.

In Pakistan and Bangladesh, democracy functions within the confines of traditional feudal structures and patronage. Elections are held, democracy and political parties flourish, but the state is fundamentally weak and corruption is rife. In Pakistan, political violence is common, and with a history of military dictatorships, the army is still feared. Interestingly, however, despite clashes amongst various ethnic elements and tensions amongst the poor, Pakistan's democratic infrastructure has, in the last decade, strengthened. Sri Lanka also boasts a democratic state, but in reality the minority Tamil population are marginalised and excluded from the decision-making process, and the country is embroiled in a civil conflict between Tamil separatists and the government.

The struggle for democracy is a long-term and highly complex process. It is characterised by popular protest, demands for wider political participation and often violence. Throughout Latin America, Africa and Asia, democratic movements were stifled by internal and external powers during the Cold War years.[23]

Latin America – From Military to Civilian Rule

Latin America is gradually emerging as a democratic zone. The years of citizen-based struggles for democracy and freedom, which reached across the world, have resulted in flourishing human rights and active civic group movements in countries such as Argentina and Mexico. However, the transition to civilian rule in many Central and Latin American societies has also been difficult and remains fragile. For years throughout the region, civil rights were abused, various forms of discrimination were rampant and economic and social conditions deteriorated. In countries such as El Salvador and Guatemala, grave violations of human rights continued under civilian governments. Disappearances and assassinations were more commonplace in formal political democracies such as Peru and Colombia than in the last years of the military dictatorships in Chile and Paraguay.

The situation is further complicated by the fact that several civilian governments face armed insurgent movements. Years of endemic and structural violence which cut through all levels of society cannot be eradicated by signatures on a declaration of peace. The guerrilla soldiers, many of whom have known nothing but fighting since childhood, have no means of entering civil society. Poverty is rampant and a black economy based on the sale of illegal drugs and arms is flourishing. The disbanded armies are reappearing on the city streets as small gangs. Violence continues to be a part of daily life, and unless the problems of economic, political and physical insecurity are addressed, it will remain a pervasive element of society for future generations.

In recent years, with the demise of the Soviet Union and the decline of socialist values, the concept of democracy has gathered momentum. Throughout Central and Eastern Europe, popular movements have developed into political parties. But despite the successes in Hungary, Poland, the Czech Republic and Russia itself, democratic rule has yet to take root and is under threat from the rise of nationalism.

Furthermore, in some cases, democracy is defined more in terms of economic liberalisation than political change. The privatisation of industry and services is occurring at such a fast pace that there has been little time for the creation of regulatory bodies to monitor changes and ensure the maintenance of service standards. In Albania, for example, where the communists of the old regime have become the liberal democrats of the new, the first half of 1997 saw the government come under violent attack for its failure to safeguard people's life savings from unsustainable and fraudulent investment schemes. Without government measures to guarantee security and a basic standard of living, the resentment towards the newly rich and disillusionment about the benefits of democracy could fuel political and social tensions.

The transition from an autocracy to a democracy requires more than election promises and ballot boxes. Key indicators include freedom of speech, a free and independent press, freedom to form political parties, freedom to vote to change the government, a justice system administered impartially, ensuring equality under the law, and a military structure whose line of command comes through the civilian government. Important institutions include democratic assemblies, civil and criminal courts and a police force, so that conflicts and disputes between individuals and groups are settled through open, prescribed procedures which everyone understands and which offer redress. Without strong public institutions able to check and balance each other's actions, democracy is easily threatened. Elections may be taking place throughout Africa, for example, but they are not yet accompanied by deeper reforms. In countries such as Kenya and Zimbabwe, freedom of speech has certainly not taken root, and too often ethnic rivalries are manipulated by those in power to undermine multi-party systems.

Africa, from Dictators to Democrats – Too Short a Step?

Between 1990 and 1991 there was a wave of multi-party elections and democratic movements across the African continent. Still the conditions are precarious. In West Africa, Niger, Gabon and Nigeria are ruled by military dictatorships, with little real evidence to show their willingness for change. In other countries, leaders have manipulated the elections, forcing opposition groups to boycott them. In Ethiopia democracy exists along ethnic lines. People vote, but there is no freedom of association for the population. Gambia, a model of multi-party democracy in the early 1990s, suffered a military coup at the hands of young soldiers in 1994. Two attempted coups in the Congo and Guinea in 1996, followed by Pierre Buyoya's successful coup in Burundi, indicate that military rule is still a potent force in African politics.[24]

Inherent in the notion of a democratic state is that the majority of the electorate believe and *trust* the government to represent their best interests and preserve their security. Yet amongst the vast majority of the world's population who have endured imperial or dictatorial rule, the government is not trusted. It is not easy to believe that elected parliamentarians will not engage in the same nepotism and corruption that their non-elected predecessors engaged in. Nor, perhaps, is it easy to be an elected parliamentarian who tries to avoid corruption and bad practice, when the system is inherently corrupt and when your supporters expect favours and rewards for giving their support. Creating institutions, forcing elections, and withholding economic aid have a limited effect in bringing long-term and deep-rooted democracy. People themselves must become active and believe in the system. In essence, for democracy to succeed, it must be accepted not just as a political system, but also as a culture of governance.

STATE FORMATION AND TRANSITION STATES

Chechen warriors performed a ritual war dance, calling for independence and promising to fight the Russians to the last drop of blood. Who were the Chechens? What did they want? In 1993, few people in Western Europe, especially politicians, knew or cared much about the tiny republic of Chechnya. The occasional television images depicting a ramshackle group of men hardly warranted any concern. Yet not long after, in 1994, Russian tanks rolled in and Chechnya exploded onto the world scene. As the death toll mounted and refugees fled, the world woke up to the realisation that many other republics of the former Soviet Union were clamouring for independence and statehood, and were willing to fight to achieve their ambitions.

From the Baltic republics of Estonia, Latvia and Lithuania to the Central Asian republics of Tajikistan, Azerbaijan, Turkmenistan, Kazakhstan, the Union of Soviet Socialist Republics seemed to unravel. But as independence was granted, local border conflicts flared up as the new states jockeyed for position and territory. Nationalistic fervour increased, causing minority ethnic groups to be ostracised and marginalised in their adopted homelands. In many places, the Russian language has been banished from official public life, as native Georgian, Azeri and a host of other regional languages have come to the fore. Yet with little provisions for minority populations, and often deliberate policies of exclusion, conflict and violence are never far away. Who fired the first shot in 1992 is unknown, but in a short space of time Georgia descended into chaos. As the minority populations, headed by the Abkhaz, demanded equality and participation in political affairs, Russian armaments arrived to assist them. Farms were destroyed and people, who only months before had thought little about their ethnicity and origins, were suddenly fleeing from one side to the other.

Elsewhere in the region, from Dagestan, with its estimated 32 distinct ethnic groups, to North Ostesia and Ingusetia, the struggle to establish new states goes on. Accustomed to central planning and directives from Moscow, most of the new states have no developed political or legislative infrastructures. Constitutions are drawn up, but are then discarded; laws are written, but often not implemented. Without support from Moscow, basic social services such as road maintenance, hospitals and schools are being neglected. Low salaries and high inflation guarantee corruption. Moreover with powerful organised crime syndicates already operating throughout the region, Moscow no longer poses the only threat. With economic and political uncertainty continuing to gnaw away at society's basic sense of security, the threat of conflict increases.

The disintegration of Yugoslavia was a direct consequence of these conditions. Yugoslavia comprised disparate and discordant social and ethnic groups, but under the command of Marshal Tito it grew into the most progressive and prosperous of the socialist states. With Tito's death in the 1980s, opposition between the groups increased. After the collapse of Soviet Russia, political leaders used nationalist sentiment to gain power. First Croatia, then Serbia declared independence. Germany, Italy and other western nations rushed to recognise them, without heeding any warning calls or concerns from minority groups in those regions. With the boundaries of the nascent states still unclear, and large numbers of Croats and Serbs living in Bosnia-Herzegovina, a struggle for control of that region, where no group had an overall majority, became inevitable.

In other parts of Central and Eastern Europe, the transition from communism to democracy has been less fraught. Despite Moscow's presence throughout the years, Mikhail Gorbachev's policies of Perestroika and Glasnost had already paved the way for reform. So without the threat of a Russian military invasion, mass public movements led by dissident leaders such as Lech Wałesa in Poland, and Vaclav Havel in Czechoslovakia called for elections and removed the communist old guard. However, ethnic minority groups straddling national borders have experienced marginalisation, and with increasing economic hardship and uncertainty amongst large cross-sections of the population, security and stability are not taken for granted.

The promotion of nationalist sentiments can strengthen a state's legitimacy, and once recognised internationally, give greater security to its community. In some instances, the combination of ethnicity and nationalism is manufactured to create the myth of a collective identity.[25] The prime function of national ideology is to justify state policy, boost morale and develop and sustain national solidarity, so that society remains cohesive. But extreme nationalism as official state policy precludes plurality and equality for all. In Sri Lanka, Sinhalese nationalist ideology led to the marginalisation of Tamils from public life. In Turkey, recent proclamations disclaiming a separate Kurd identity, language and ethnicity have served to entrench positions even further. In both cases, as the minority groups use violence and confrontation to assert their rights, the fabric of society is actually pulled apart. Invariably as nationalist sentiment flourishes, so do the divisions in society.

REJECTING SECULARISM

Perhaps the greatest shock to western liberal observers in recent years has been the rejection of western democratic ideals and secularism in favour of religious states. From Iran in 1979 to Turkey in 1996, support for Sharia law as the basis of government has strengthened in numerous countries. With Islamic fervour growing, other religious groups have also called for a reassertion of their values and principles.

In India the destruction of the Ayodhya temple by Hindu extremists, the resurgence of Hindu militancy and its mobilisation by political forces within the nationalist Bharatiya Janata Party (BJP) demonstrate the fragility and strengths of secular traditions of the country. Elsewhere in the sub-continent, Pakistan, Bangladesh and Sri Lanka still resort to religion as a means of political power while alienating minorities and entrenching divisions. In Israel and Palestine, hard-line Muslims and Jews have both been actively condemning the peace process and causing rifts within their own communities.

Religion and politics have always been a potent mix and the cause of numerous wars. But with the advent of Marxism and the Cold War, the threat of religion was eclipsed by other ideologies. Now it seems that religion, be it Islam, Christianity, Judaism, Hinduism or Buddhism, is forcing its way back into national and international politics, with the potential to challenge and even undermine secular states and weak democracies.

Ideological Conflicts

The Oxford Dictionary defines the term 'ideology' as:

1. the system of ideas at the basis of an economic or political theory;
2. the manner of thinking characteristic of a class or individual;
3. visionary speculation.[26]

In the twentieth century, the principal ideological conflict has been between communism and capitalism, and their interpretations of society and the human condition. The socialist/communist ideal of a society of equals sharing material goods and working for the improvement of society as a whole enjoyed widespread support throughout the world for many years. It spawned a multitude of peaceful and armed socialist and communist insurgency movements fighting capitalism and military rule. But with the collapse of the Soviet Union and the demise of Maoism in China, Marxist idealism and the dream of a communist Utopia have faded.

At first glance in the early post-Cold War days, the demise of communism was equated with the victory of capitalism and the liberal democratic model. For many, Francis Fukuyama's paper 'The End of History'[27] convincingly argued that the lack of alternative models meant that despite its shortcomings, the western model of a liberal democratic state had won. It was the best system of governance that humanity could devise, and it was universally desired. Perhaps it was a comforting thought to believe that the entire world wanted to emulate western-style governance. But it did not last very long. Even in the western world new political ideologies are emerging. By putting aside conventional left- and right-wing attitudes, a new realism is beginning to dominate politics.[28] In effect, it appears that the end of communism is heralding the end of conservative capitalism as well. Furthermore, in their rejection of overarching ideological systems, i.e. left versus right, people are creating more disparate and issue-based value systems. So, for example, animal rights activists compete with anti-abortionists and environmentalists for a space in the central political arena.

In extreme cases, violence and terrorism erupt when these new forces clash with the status quo. In the US elements within the anti-abortion lobby have attacked clinics and killed medical staff. Elsewhere in the US the bombing of a government building in Oklahoma has focused attention on new internal threats. These groups may be small and disparate, but their access to weapons and use of information technology to communicate and network with each other does not bode well for the future.

Militias or Freedom-fighters[29]

In the aftermath of the Oklahoma bombing, when sympathy for federal bureaucrats should have been at its highest, the *Los Angeles Times* took a poll. Its results showed that up to 45 per cent of the population believed that the government posed a threat to their constitutional rights. In Indianapolis, the American Justice Federation, a loose network of unorganised militias, boasts a nationwide membership of three million. Some estimates suggest that up to 27 per cent of the population would be willing to take up arms against the federal government if it posed a threat to their liberties. The fall of the one great enemy – the Soviet Union – and increasing disillusionment with their own government for its inability to defend their rights and needs have allowed these militias to emerge to fill a void. They regard themselves as freedom-fighters willing to use arms in their war against state control.

Across the Pacific in Australia, armed militia groups carry out military manoeuvres and exercises in their preparations for a decisive battle to protect their country and heritage. Amongst them is AUSI Scouts (Australians United for Survival and Individual Freedom), a private army of Christian fundamentalists claiming up to 3,000 supporters nation-wide. They are loosely networked with other groups in Australia, and have links with radical right-wing groups in the US and elsewhere. Though disparate and often limited in membership, these groups share a common agenda: opposition to the extension of the federal government, the encroachment of international banking and business and, of course, gun control. They themselves are well armed and appear to have little regard for state and national laws. Moreover, they are willing to take up arms if they believe their civil liberties are threatened.

In poorer countries it has become increasingly apparent that new ideologies are emerging to articulate the experience of poverty, inequality and despair that is still at the root of such conflicts.[30] As mentioned above, religious ideology has also come to the fore. Religious ideology lacks the clarity and direction that defined communism and capitalism. There is no obvious centre. Instead, the movements are cloaked in secrecy, and there is no normative or formulaic structure to define the groups. It is a potent mix of spirituality, morality, sense of identity and hope in this life and the afterlife that has bred success for religious movements and militants. In the Middle East and North Africa, Islamic ideology is used to counter westernisation. Just as communism addressed the inequalities in society, so Islam is being used as a vehicle to gather support against ruling governments in countries such as Egypt, Pakistan and Indonesia.

Identity Conflicts

Identity is an intrinsic element of the 'self', encompassing the psychological, physical, social and spiritual sense of a person's existence. Any threat to this core sense of identity can override rational thought and reasoning. In other words, a sense of security based on a distinctive identity, a wider social recognition of that identity and effective participation in social, economic and political processes are the basic needs of all humanity.[31] The denial of such needs can lead to a feeling of victimisation and also to conflict. But how is that sense of self or identity defined? And how does one person's self-perceptions match their neighbour's perceptions of them?

Ethnicity is a variant on identity, which in turn is dynamic and ephemeral. In many ways an attempt to define the term 'ethnicity' reveals the degree of complexity which surrounds this issue. Ethnicity can refer to a person's origins: Kurd, Turk or Arab, for example. It can refer to a person's physical features: dark or pale skin. It can also refer to economic status, as groups that are particularly close in other ways will often distinguish themselves by emphasising the disparity in wealth and power. In Rwandese, for example, the term 'Tutsi' means 'aristocrat', while 'Hutu' means 'peasant or cattle herder'. Yet over time, they have come to distinguish ethnicity.

Ethnicity can be derived from one's religion: Jewish versus Christian, Muslim or Hindu. Despite predictions that the influence of religion would diminish as societies grew more sophisticated, religion continues to provide a primary source of meaning and identity to many people, and in some cases encourages followers to believe that they are special, different and often better than others. Judaism makes claims of exclusivity and accentuates the myth of the 'chosen' people, while Christianity and Islam perpetuate the idea that non-believers will suffer after death.

Yet, no matter how communal or group identity is defined, it is an intrinsic and powerful form of social expression. Edward Azar gives much credence to the role of *group identity*, stating that it is difficult to measure insecurity or injustice in isolation from ethnic or communal structures. So for example, it is easier and more natural for an innocent man accused of a crime against the government of Turkey to articulate his sense of injustice by thinking 'I am a Kurd, therefore I am being treated unjustly' than for him to dissociate his identity from his feelings of injustice. Furthermore, Azar suggests that since the emergence of the nation-state, ethnic and group identities have been subsumed by national identities.[32] The concept of a single national identity suppresses communal group identity based on religion, culture, ethnicity or race. In the international arena of global politics and state-based institutions, this fundamental oversight of communal groupings is now taking its toll.

Globalisation and the threat of cultural homogenisation is also undermining people's identities and creating insecurity. As cultural values are becoming blurred, people within different cultural and ethnic groups are seeking to retain their unique traditions, beliefs, languages and social values. If an ethnic or cultural group feel their value system and traditions are being swept aside, they become more defensive and determined to keep their distance and sense of separateness. As a result, the reassertion of group identity is proving to be a potent by-product of the globalisation process. This is being exacerbated in many cases by advances in modern technology. Although it is often argued that the radio, television and, more recently, the Internet would precipitate a kind of cultural homogeneity, in reality the developments are more complex. Increasingly the same media are used by ethnic minorities to promote their own values. During the Iranian revolution, for example, recorded messages by Ayatollah Khomeini were smuggled into Iran and used to mobilise the poor urban and rural populations. During the early 1990s in Rwanda, radio was the main channel of communication for extremist groups. Throughout the Bosnian war, Serbian television broadcast an unending barrage of propaganda against the Muslims.

Yet it would be wrong to assume that all multi-ethnic or plural societies suffer ethnic tension or violence. Indeed, for the majority, their plurality is a source of creativity. However, the stability of a plural state depends to a large extent on the stratification and levels of cohabitation between the ethnic communities within that society.[33]

In apartheid South Africa, there was a distinct, vertical hierarchical 'ethnic' division. The minority group occupied all the top positions in the political, legal, social, economic and cultural spheres, while the blacks and 'coloured' people (of mixed race or Indian origin) were very clearly subordinate to them. In contrast, in Sri Lanka and Israel, a majority population dominates and oppresses a minority. (See Figure 2.1.)

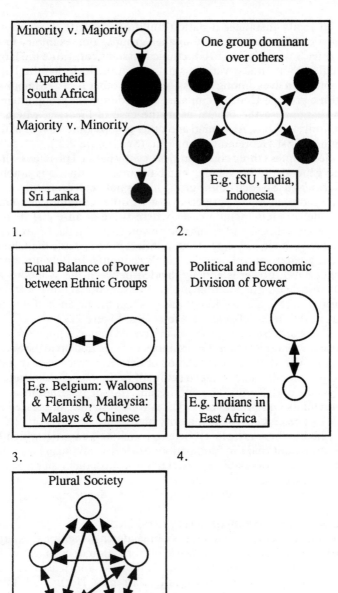

Figures 2.1–5 Ethnicity Diagrams

In many instances a nation-building majority population is balanced by a number of smaller groups. For example, in the former Soviet Union (fSU), ethnic Russians constitute the largest single group amidst various smaller groups. In India, the Hindu population lives among a cross-section of other races, religious and ethnic groups. Conflict can arise if the dominant group attempts to marginalise the others, as in the case of Georgia, where the minority Abkhaz, Armenian and other groups joined forces in their fight against Georgian nationalism. (See Figure 2.2.)

Sometimes ethnic communities occupy parallel positions within the general public sphere, but have internal divisions amongst themselves. So each ethnic group has its political, economic, social elite representing its interests vis-à-vis other communities. Other parallel models include cases where there is an equal division between political and economic power. In Malaysia, for example, Malayans have a monopoly on political power, while the Chinese exert greater control over the state's economy. In Belgium, on the other hand, power is equally divided between the Walloons and Flemish, with the latter having greater functional powers and the former, a stronger territorial base. When the balance of power is equal, the threat of conflict is less. (See Figure 2.3.)

There are also cases where an oppressed minority population has greater economic power. For example, in the period up to the Second World War, the Jewish population of Eastern Europe were resented for their wealth and financial acumen. In the east African states of Uganda and Kenya, the immigrant Indian population as the merchants and professional classes were resented, oppressed and finally persecuted by the majority black state. (See Figure 2.4.)

Finally, there are plural societies, such as Tanzania, which has no dominant majority population. Society is not stagnant, rather the dynamics of relations between the groups, maintains a general status quo. Social and economic inequality may exist, but they are not imposed by one group upon another. (See Figure 2.5.)

MANIFESTATIONS OF IDENTITY CONFLICTS
Conflict can erupt when there is a breakdown of legitimate political order as well as a collective sense of frustration or even fear within a population. But the build-up to the fear and frustration can occur in many ways. In Rwanda, extremist Hutus and Tutsis carried out a campaign of hatred. Over a period of two years the Hutu extremists drew on old 'ethnic' rivalries and social imbalances to denounce the Tutsi minority. The Tutsi extremists countered with their own propaganda and the culmination was that the peoples of one state which spoke the same language, practised the same religion and inter-married, gradually polarised into two distinct 'ethnic' camps.

In Israel, a different form of polarisation has taken root. Israelis and Palestinians live and work amongst each other, yet there exists a barrier of mistrust, fear and ignorance. Each group has demonised and to some extent dehumanised the other. Young Israelis who join the army are forced to think of Palestinians as 'the enemy' who wish to reclaim the whole of Israel. Similarly, Palestinians, having lived through decades of occupation and grinding poverty, look upon Israelis as the illegal occupiers of their lands. The Oslo peace process may be resurrected successfully,[34] but it will still take many years before real trust replaces fear and familiarity replaces ignorance.

Conflict often breaks out when one side has the capacity to incite violence, while the other has neither the means of defending itself, nor the means to counter-attack. This was the case in Bosnia, where the Serbs had military power, and the Muslims had few resources.[35] The real struggle was for power and territory, but rekindling old animosities was a powerful means of politicising the differences that had lain dormant for years and mobilising a wider Serb population.

For the Muslims, many of whom had never considered their origins to be different from those of the Serbs (primarily because their ethnic and racial roots are Serbo-Croat), the onslaught of violence and ethnic cleansing compelled them to forge stronger links with other Muslims and break existing socio-economic ties with Serbs and Croats. Furthermore, the combined factors of being labelled so strongly as 'Muslims' and not receiving the necessary assistance from the West eventually drove them towards the Islamic countries of the Middle East for support and legitimacy. In other words, the war not only resurrected differences which had been buried for years, but also generated a new sense of identity and division.

Most ethnic or minority groups today have a substantial international or transnational component which can also result in conflict. This may be due to cross-border affiliations or the existence of diasporas which provide support for these movements. In the case of Northern Ireland financial support from a vast community of Irish-Americans has sustained the Provisional Irish Republican Army (IRA) far beyond its traditional grassroots support base. Similarly the Liberation Tamil Tigers of Eelam (LTTE) of Sri Lanka are strengthened through a network of international Tamil groups, which are more powerful than traditional grassroots LTTE supporters in Sri Lanka itself.

In the case of the Kurds, who occupy land straddling the borders of Turkey, Iraq and Iran, the cross-border links have enhanced and politicised their ethnicity. Marginalised and persecuted by each of the states, the 20 million Kurds have long fought to maintain their cultural values and language, and dream of an independent state. The need for a nation-state with defined boundaries and recognised social and political institutions arises from their lack of legitimacy in the social, political and economic landscapes of the states they currently live in. In addition, since the international system is based on state participation, Kurds lack representation in structures such as the UN. In other words, so long as they remain a minority ethnic group within other nation-states, they will remain marginalised and powerless. Thus they use their ethnic origins and history as a basis for political claims.[36]

One of the greatest threats to international security is that of trans-border ethnic conflicts spreading. But often the international community remains disinterested for too long, and until it is too late. In Central Africa, for example, the conflict in Rwanda was to a degree mirrored in Burundi, as extremist militia groups plundered and slaughtered innocent civilians. The flow of refugees into neighbouring Zaire, Uganda and Tanzania exported the violence to those states. By November 1996, the presence of the Hutu-based extremist Interahamwe in Zaire, combined with anti-Tutsi sentiment on the part of the Zairian government, unleashed further conflict. Evidence indicates that Laurent Kabila, erstwhile rebel leader, now president of the new Democratic Republic of Congo (former Zaire), was supported by the Rwandan and Ugandan armies. At the time of writing there is no outright warfare but much evidence of mass killings of Hutu refugees.

Too often the lack of international interest or concern in the cause of persecuted or minority groups results in desperate acts of aggression in the wider international arena. In recent years, many have chosen a more high-profile expression of anger: taking western hostages as a means of attracting the attention of more powerful nations. Since 1994, Kashmiri militant separatists have killed innocent foreign hostages, and members of the Free Papua Movement of Irian Jaya in Indonesia have also gained publicity through hostage-taking. The Revolutionary United Front of Sierra Leone (RUF/SL) entered into dialogue with the international community after taking and releasing 25 innocent hostages. In December 1996, the siege of the Japanese embassy in Peru propelled the cause of the rebel Tupac Amaru Marxist movement onto the world stage. These are warnings to the international community. Ignoring the plight of minorities today may also mean increasing insecurity for foreigners abroad, or indeed desperate acts of terrorism in London, Paris, Tokyo and Washington tomorrow.

Finally, of growing importance will be new types of *racial* conflicts likely to emerge in areas with large and growing numbers of immigrants and refugees. The numbers heading westwards are minimal compared to the number of refugees that exist throughout the developing world. Yet immigration issues are already provoking intense debate in the US and Europe, with demands for various control policies to stem the tide of new arrivals. In the 1980s extreme right-wing parties were able to establish themselves in Germany, Austria and France and achieve worrying electoral success. Furthermore, although the melting-pot myth still runs strong in American national rhetoric and is often emulated in other western countries, there is no doubt that tensions and prejudices are emerging amongst the different minority groups. In Britain, for example, there is growing evidence of violent attacks between members of the Indian Sikh and Muslim communities. In America itself, anti-immigration sentiment runs high in a number of states, resulting in legislation which excludes illegal immigrants from education and health care. The lack of education or job opportunities coupled with social and political injustices could eventually manifest itself in inter-ethnic disputes and more aggressive nationalistic tendencies.

The Changing Nature of Contemporary Warfare

Much has changed since the heyday of the Cold War when superpower states vying for influence world-wide equipped favoured governments and guerrilla groups with all the necessary military equipment, training and financial aid. From Mobuto Sese Seko to the Shah of Iran, regional power bases were established. Politically and economically underdeveloped states boasted powerful armies and superior weapons technology. These highly centralised states may have used different methods of controlling internal insurrections, but in essence they depended on external patronage to sustain their armies. Now that the rationale for that patronage has disappeared, once powerful armies have fragmented or collapsed, giving rise to new sources of insecurity.

In short, five broad trends for the future of warfare can be identified; first, the privatisation of state armies; second, the growth of militias and local warlords; third, the deliberate targeting of civilian populations and children; fourth, narco-guerrillas and criminality; and finally, the re-emergence of mercenary soldiers.

Privatisation of State Armies

In the absence of external patronage, conscript armies, or what is left of them, are known to sell their arms, equipment or services to the highest bidder. In Ethiopia even officers were found to be selling arms and ammunition during the closing years of the war. In the former Zaire, with its sprawling territories, some military commanders ran what was akin to personal fiefdoms. The soldiers were not paid regular salaries, but instead were encouraged to loot and pillage local villages, demand 'contributions' at arbitrary roadblocks and commit sexual violence against local women.[37] In Liberia, Charles Taylor used local logging concessions to finance his troops. In Sierra Leone, the control of diamond concessions has been a major factor in the war. In Angola, as UNITA struggles to maintain its control over diamond mines and ivory smuggling, the country is left in a state of neither peace nor war. So it appears that as the military units or rebel factions find alternative means of sustaining themselves, they fragment, transforming into private militias, with local commanders taking on leadership and decision-making.

Mobuto's Hollow Forces

At the height of President Mobuto's power, Zaire's military prowess was hailed amongst the elite of Africa. Yet fearing internal strife, Mobuto's strategy was to disempower the national army, reduce its numbers to only 20,000 and provide little equipment or training. Instead he concentrated on creating a series of covert special strike forces, formed and dissolved in quick succession. In addition, he commandeered no fewer than six security forces, with the men chosen for their unquestioning loyalty to the president. By maintaining this degree of fragmentation, he ensured that none of the units could develop their own independent power bases.

However, the end of the Cold War reduced Zaire's strategic value in the global arena, and Mobuto became increasingly isolated. The Rwandan refugee camps in Zaire ensured a continued flow of aid and provisions into the country, but the state structure was cracking under the weight of decades of corruption and mismanagement. The system eventually backfired and collapsed, as regional units became increasingly distant from the centre, and the undisciplined and poorly equipped army disintegrated in the onslaught of Laurent Kabila's few, but well trained forces.

Warlords and Militias

Complex political, social and economic undercurrents have affected military strategies of warfare in the 1990s, and often, the semblance of anarchy is a part of that doctrine.[38] To an outsider the violence and war-ridden societies of Sierra Leone and Liberia may appear to be anarchic and degenerate. There seems to be little order in the chaos, no discipline or control in the military ranks. Across the conflict-ridden regions of Africa, distinguishing between insurgency and counter-insurgency movements, soldiers and rebels is increasingly blurred by the realities on the ground. Without the help of a patron state, many governments are unable to supply basic provisions, clothing, food or medication for their troops. So the troops have to fend for themselves. The soldiers of the Sierra Leone national army, for example, were labelled 'sobel': soldiers by day and rebels by night as they looted homes and raided villages. The terrorising of villages and civilian communities is not an arbitrary side-effect of contemporary warfare, however. It is part of a wider military doctrine which has been developed by rebel leaders over the years. From the point of recruitment, to training and initiating attacks, the strategies of today are an amalgamation of traditional tribal warfare, Cold War counter-insurgency techniques and the field experiences of military leaders such as Yoweri Museveni, Jonas Savimbi and Charles Taylor.[39]

The objective in most cases is to destabilise communities, pitting civilians against each other, compelling them to take sides and so feed and fuel the conflicting parties. By introducing just a few individuals into a large community to create violence and terror against one ethnic group or faction, the seeds of mistrust and tension can be sown. In Liberia, atrocities were deliberately highlighted and exposed to the media in order to inspire fear in the wider populace. In part, both Charles Taylor and his rival Prince Johnson aimed to mobilise support by generating absolute terror so that people would not even contemplate resistance. But also it was a means of getting people to flee their homes, so that looting by soldiers becomes much easier. Moreover, by generating a mass of displaced peoples, the militias ensured a flow of international aid. As camps form, food and medical aid flow in, and militias take control of policing the populations. Through elaborate systems of 'taxation', extortion and bribery, they siphon off enough supplies to strengthen their numbers. With so many civilians – many of them young men with little to do, disillusioned, angered and desperate to flee the squalor – the camps become ideal recruiting grounds for the militia. Consequently, the system of international aid and relief may inadvertanly oil the wheels in the continuing cycle of conflict.

The Use of Children

Another characteristic of contemporary civil wars is the use of children.[40] This not only changes the nature of the wars being fought, but also the social landscape of the future. The use of young recruits and children as young as eight has been evident in a number of long-term conflicts, especially where there is a shortage of manpower. Ethiopia, Sudan, Iran and Sri Lanka are just some of the states in which children have been used in warfare. Although historically children have been present in military encampments, it is only in recent years that children have fought on the frontline. This is largely due to the availability of cheap, light and easy to use automatic weapons. Moreover, children are more easy to recruit. When communities have been disrupted and families separated, young children are enticed into joining militia units with the promise of stability and a new 'family'. Those who are orphaned have little choice but to follow guerrilla forces, while others may be put under peer pressure and the promise of excitement and adventure.

Child soldiers are, by and large, more obedient and disciplined than their older counterparts. They tend to follow directions precisely, rarely being open to compromise. In cases where executions are planned, but where adults are unwilling to undertake the task, children are often more willing to comply. They have a limited sense of absolute morals and can be easily brainwashed. They lack a developed notion of proportion, so they are more willing to commit acts of extreme violence. Often children treat war as a game, so they do not know when to stop, nor when to withdraw if a situation is untenable. Thus in some cases if caught in a conventional battle children may be slaughtered, but in other cases they can be devastatingly brutal. Another dimension of child soldiers is their relative cheapness. In Liberia, it is alleged that children were paid in cocaine and marijuana. Sometimes they are content with simple treats such as a ride on a motorbike or new clothes.

All in all, the long-term social and psychological impact of having generations of children scarred by war or trained to kill and torture is yet to be fully realised. But there is little doubt of the damage that is being done. More ominously, there is little doubt that the use of children could become an increasingly common feature of modern warfare.

Narco-Guerrillas

As the rules and actors of war change, a number of even more contentious issues have entered the equation. The freedom-fighters, ideologues and opportunists of the Cold War years have much the same aims as before, but in adjusting to new economic and political realities they have had to adapt their strategies and take on new allies. In Latin America and Colombia in particular, a new breed of narco-guerrillas has emerged.[41] With their traditional financial lifelines practically severed, the revolutionary Marxist guerrillas have turned to the drug barons and cocaine producers of their own country for support. In return for safe passage through the jungles and across the borders, the guerrillas receive a percentage for each kilo of cocaine smuggled. They also provide protection for the clandestine laboratories and production facilities, and are willing to fight the Colombian officials and drug enforcement agents who come their way. Through coercion, fear or enticement, they continue to recruit from amongst the poor and marginalised rural communities.

Much the same goes on across the world in Afghanistan, where the trade in opium and heroin flourishes. Further afield in Laos and Myanmar (Burma), ethnic warlords who fought the Burmese army now collude with corrupt Burmese generals in running heroin supplies through jungle routes.[42] Like their counterparts in Africa, those who lead are busy amassing their personal wealth, while still peddling the myth of a better world and greater opportunities for their followers.

Mercenaries

The disintegration of state armies has also led to a resurgence of mercenaries and bounty hunters in most conflict regions. With no interest or concern for the countries in which they fight, these groups rarely have an incentive to end the conflict. From Sierra Leone to Angola, Sri Lanka, the Middle East and Papua New Guinea, the presence of mercenaries, heavily armed, highly trained, protecting and preserving ramshackle regimes or factions, can not only prolong but also intensify conflicts. Furthermore, with an avaricious eye on diamonds, gold, oil and other precious materials, such groups have an interest in developing local bases and effectively recolonising entire regions. Yet they invest nothing and have no roots or ties in the regions, so for them too peace and orderly governance bring few rewards.

Have Gun Will Travel: Executive Outcomes: Private Security or the Dogs of War[43]

Eeben Barlow, Chief Executive of Executive Outcomes (EO), prefers to regard his company as a 'team of trouble-shooters, marketing a strategy of recovery to failing governments around the world. He imagines EO as a kind of advance team for the UN, his rationale being that if you cannot keep peace, there is no peace.' There may be a certain logic to his views, and certainly a vision of paid and dedicated UN soldiers, rather than the arbitrary mix of multinational forces which come together under the UN banner in emergency situations is not entirely unrealistic. But that is a far cry from the reality that EO seems to be.

Formed in 1991 by an assortment of veteran apartheid soldiers, spies and 'security' specialists, EO's first contract came from a partnership of the oil giants Gulf and Chevron for the protection of their oilfields in Angola.

By 1993, the Angolan government had hired them to train its soldiers and help crush the UNITA rebel forces. In 1995 they appeared in Sierra Leone, siding with the military government against the RUF/SL. Critics argue that EO is no better than a latterday colonial power in Africa, willing to fight for anyone who pays the most. In Angola, they were said to fight on both sides at various times.

Certainly, there is little doubt that the organisation's prime objective is to make money. Their contract with the Angolan government was said to be worth US$ 40 million. In Sierra Leone they negotiated highly lucrative diamond concessions. The company's strategy is two-fold. On the one hand, it appears to offer security and to 'legitimate' regimes, particularly in areas of rich mineral resources and lucrative pickings. On the other hand, they ensure that the resources are available for the requisitioning of weapons and armament for the company and the regime. Thus, the economic interests of both parties are tied together.

Membership of EO is up to 2,500 with active recruitment around the world. In 1996 a number of veteran Serb soldiers arrived in the former Zaire to train the beleaguered military. In recent years the company has branched out in a variety of directions, marketing itself as a mining company, with interests in tourism and, of course, security. However, there is little doubt that funding comes primarily from their mercenary activities in Africa.

The company is said to have contracts in Kenya, Malawi, Mozambique, Somalia, Sudan and Uganda. Ironically, they are all member states of the Organisation for African Unity (OAU) and signatories to a resolution outlawing the use of mercenaries. Even the OAU has shown interest in hiring the firm to manage its peacekeeping operations.

There is no accountability to any well-developed code of conduct for internal conflicts. International human rights and humanitarian laws are ignored by all sides. States and militias kill, poison and slaughter with impunity. The protagonists of modern-day conflicts are the beneficiaries of this new war economy. For many there is no real interest or incentive to stop.

The Intractable Nature of Internal Conflicts

So is the stand-off between Angolan rebels and the government a question of justice and fair governance, or is it about who controls the diamond mines? Is the Palestine–Israel conflict about religion, territory, power or identity? Was Chechnya solely a conflict over governance? Was Bosnia solely the resurgence of a long-standing ethnic feud? From the discussion above it is clear that *rigid* typologies are not sufficient to explain or understand conflicts. Nor are the motives and incentives of the disputants always evident. The final expression of violence may be between one 'ethnic' group and another; or guerrilla leaders may mobilise forces with ideological rhetoric, but there are other forces at work too. As a conflict spreads, these causes become increasingly more entangled and complex, making the conflict all-encompassing and intractable.

When disputes escalate, new lines of demarcation are drawn, and often historical events are juxtaposed with contemporary feelings of insecurity and injustice, thereby fuelling the need for confrontation. In the former Yugoslavia, for example, on the one hand, Muslims were branded as 'Turks', a reference to the brutal conquering Ottoman Empire of previous centuries; while on the other hand, by virtue of being Muslim, they were linked to the stereotypical image of fundamentalist Middle Eastern Muslims. Thus many of the Serbs were led to believe that a Muslim-led Bosnian state would be a dictatorial theocracy, which had to be resisted at all costs. Furthermore, beyond the historical and cultural animosities there also lay a level of present-day economic envy, as Bosnian Muslims were the most wealthy, educated and urbane of the different groups. So in part, the propaganda used to galvanise popular Serb support for the conflict was a promise of a better and wealthier existence, without the Muslims.

Azar suggests that social conflicts often become even more complex and protracted as external factors begin to enter the dynamics.[44] Regional and international powers intervene, taking sides and further exacerbating existing relations. In cases such as Angola, Mozambique and Afghanistan, local conflicts were hijacked to become pawns in superpower games. The diaspora can play a prominent role in funding and encouraging a non-compromising stance. As indicated even humanitarian aid, though necessary, can have a negative impact on the conflict. Finally, the ready supply of arms is a guaranteed means of fuelling a conflict. On the one hand, the availability of arms and ammunition provides extra strength and is itself a reason to continue fighting. While, on the other hand, the spread of arms sows the seeds for a culture of violence. So even if there is a collective will to stop a war, the daily violence and killing continue and can become a major obstacle in peacemaking.

The impact of protracted conflicts on economic development in many poor and less developed countries destroys the state's ability to meet the needs of its citizens, even those who support the system. Weapons procurement and defence strategies surpass any plans for development and economic growth. The lack of resources, food, employment and goods intensifies competition amongst social groups, and this in turn intensifies the level of conflict and violence.

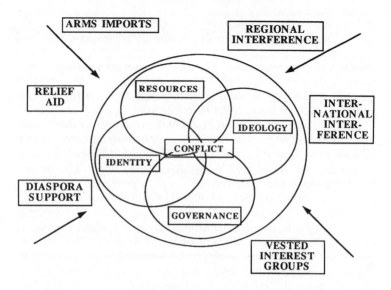

Figure 2.6 The Intractable Nature of Internal Conflicts

No individual can escape the impact of war. Anyone who remains neutral risks being branded a collaborator. Orderly social existence is replaced by a culture of violence, fuelled by the need to defend, take revenge or take pre-emptive action. Increased polarisation between communities results in a fatalistic attitude towards the conflict. The initial political dispute, which may still be the rhetoric of the leadership, is overshadowed by a real fear for physical survival and a profound belief that compromise is impossible.

Conclusion

Yet conflicts do stop, and even after decades of war there can be peace. Furthermore, it is our belief that conflicts can also be prevented. But the question is, how? What are the factors that need to be addressed? Arguably, carefully constructed typologies and frameworks bear little resemblance to the realities in the field. But by analysing the structure of a conflict and its political economy and carefully determining the beneficiaries of war, as well as identifying the protagonists, the issues at stake, the historical and geopolitical context, the economic factors and social and military dilemmas, opportunities for peacemaking and resolution can be opened up. In the following chapters we explore how.

CHAPTER 3

From Early Warning to Early Action

In the beginning, war was only a word. It did not have substance for me. Journalists and political leaders used the word occasionally at first, then more frequently. But people did not utter the word because no one believed it could really happen. In the long phase of preparations and denial the substance began to slowly fill that ugly word until it became fat and real, like an insatiable dangerous animal.
(Slavenka Drakulic, *Letters from Zagreb on the Nature of War*)[1]

Introduction

War does not erupt overnight. No matter how disparate or complex a society may be, *communal* violence does not erupt unprovoked. Inevitably, it is the manifestation of *accumulated* hostility and aggression between opposing sides. But how does this aggression accumulate? How can we tell whether a disagreement between two communities, or a benign form of ethnic rivalry, is actually transforming into a more serious conflict? What indications can be found? What factors eventually trigger violence? What, if anything, can be done, by whom and at what stage to avert a crisis? In essence, what kind of *early warning signals* should be looked for, and what kind of *early preventive action* could be taken to avert violence?

Early warning is in many ways the cornerstone of preventive action. It can be defined as the capacity for *information gathering* and *analysis* with the *purpose of providing strategic options for preventive action* and/or an *informed, appropriate response*.[2] Early warning systems already exist for natural disasters such as floods, hurricanes, volcanoes and even earthquakes. There are also sophisticated systems geared to identifying potential refugee flows during a crisis. With such systems in place, in theory, the authorities responsible for assisting victims and managing crises have the opportunity to develop contingency plans. Ideally, therefore, when a warning is given, the plans go into operation, caring for and saving more victims than would otherwise be possible.

When it comes to conflict and war however, early warning is concerned with *forecasting* the potential for the escalation of inter- and intra-state conflicts. Predictions about crises would be part of the system, but the aim is to help avert the initial development of a crisis. Contingency planning for victims is also part of the system, but the prime focus is *victim prevention.* So a successful conflict early warning system would be one which through its warnings could generate timely action to avert violence. In other words, such a system would itself be an early action tool, and would be of immense strategic importance.

In this chapter we examine the ways in which conflict early warning and intervention systems could be developed. At this stage it is important to emphasise that much of what is discussed relates to constructed models which do not always reflect every reality on the ground. But they are still useful in providing a frame of reference and structure upon which to work.

We begin by using a model scaling the continuum between peace and war to show how there are a number of stages between the two extremes. Then by taking a closer look at the various social indicators, we can see how the interaction and combination of factors can contribute to the build-up of communal tensions and the outbreak of violence. This is followed by a discussion on the components necessary to devise an early warning system; the ways in which different sectors of society could contribute to the development of such a system; and a range of factors which can help or hinder the efficiency of such a system.

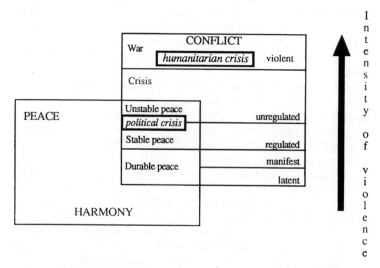

Figure 3.1 From Harmony to Warfare: The Continuum of Peace and Conflict

The Continuum of Conflict

In considering an early warning system it is important to recognise that war and peace exist at opposite ends of the same scale.[3] So, in the first instance, it is useful to be aware of the various levels and intensities of conflict and violence that can exist between parties. In general terms, it is possible to identify five different stages of conflict and hostility.

Durable Peace

It is rare to find societies which exist in *complete harmony*, with no social tensions or conflict whatsoever.[4] More often than not, tensions exist between the rich and the poor, between competing political parties and ideologies, and between various interest groups. But this conflict is not in itself a sign of *impending violence*. In essence, there is *durable peace*, that is, the ruling elite have political legitimacy, and values and interests are pursued within a legitimate framework. Disputes are settled through designated institutions and structures, or in extreme cases through peaceful demonstrations or actions. The possibility of physical conflict or repression is virtually non-existent, and military force is not needed to guarantee security. So despite the conflicts of interest, the *intensity of hostility* and the degree of aggression manifested between groups are not high.

Stable Peace

In many instances, although the levels of hostility are higher, and groups are mutually distrustful of one another, there is still a state of *stable peace*. However, there may be a *political crisis* as tensions rise and extremist or fringe political movements emerge, emphasising the differences between groups. Inflammatory public declarations and speeches can lead to a further polarisation of the society. The relationship between the ruling political elite and opposition groups or segments of society can become more fraught. Extra-parliamentary groups become more active, promoting a clear political agenda. Minor degrees of violence and oppression can occur. But still, the rule of law stands firm and is respected by all sides.

Unstable Peace

A state of *unstable peace* is reached as communication between parties decreases. Suspicions and tension mount and though there may be little actual violence, there is nothing to guarantee peace. In domestic situations, unstable peace can occur where a government maintains power through the overt use of coercion and repression and outlaws any form of dissent. Alternatively, if inflammatory rhetoric increases, gradually group divisions become articulated through mainstream political parties and processes.

Parties may form on the basis of ethnicity, race or religion. Sporadic violence may break out between social groups or against established authorities. Accusations of corruption and fraud become rife and demonstrations may degenerate into violence. Charges of torture and death while in police custody increase, as can political assassinations, intimidation and acts of political terrorism.

In some cases a state of anomie[5] also becomes evident as groups become increasingly isolated and disengaged. Previously existing social institutions and structures of governance may lose their perceived legitimacy. Mutual intimidation or the repression of the weaker side by the stronger becomes more widespread. In Bosnia, the early incidences of ethnic cleansing and intimidation of the Muslims by the Serbs are an apt example of this state. In essence this is the stage at which violence enters the equation and becomes an accepted means of articulating anger. It is also the genesis of what can later become the dehumanisation and demonisation of one side by the other, as the parties move away from a common framework of understanding of what is right and wrong, moral or immoral, acceptable or unacceptable social behaviour.

Crisis – Low-Intensity Conflict

A *crisis point* is reached when rival groups or dissidents take up arms and engage in physical hostilities. But still the conflict is limited to a recognised group within a confined geographical area. Though this may be defined as low-intensity conflict with little impact on the country at large, there is no doubt that for the parties involved, extra-judicial killings, rebel attacks, torture and subjugation are common occurrences. But as the conflict spreads, state security and military forces engage in armed confrontation. Military curfews may be imposed, restricting movement, political gatherings, assemblies and freedom of speech. It is the beginnings of a *humanitarian crisis*, when private militias form, massacres occur and people begin to flee their homes. As law and order break down, the security forces take on political power and act with increasing impunity.

Civil War – High-Intensity Conflict

Gradually as the whole country becomes engulfed in violence, *high-intensity* or *full-scale civil war* emerges. The entire population may become polarised along group lines, each claiming its own rights and individual identity. The tide of displaced people swells as homes are destroyed and the economy reaches breaking point. All forms of law and order are flouted as militias, rebels and death squads roam the streets. In Burundi since 1994, for example, as the government disintegrated, extremist rebels committed massacres with impunity, and the Tutsi-dominated military took control, also committing gross human rights abuses, massacres and terror. In this stage of conflict, civilians become the pawns of opposing parties, and rival governments may form calling for foreign military aid or intervention. This level of violence may become the status quo for years.

In reality, of course, the demarcations between the various stages of conflict are rarely so clear. Often in essentially peaceful societies, there are elements of communal violence or low-intensity conflict, as in the case of Britain and the Northern Ireland conflict, or Spain and the Basque conflict. Alternatively, in situations of war, there are often pockets of peace or even periods of relative calm. Furthermore, more often than not, a country may experience varying levels of conflict simultaneously in different regions or amongst different communities. For example, in November 1996, the people of eastern Zaire were, to all intents and purposes, in the grips of full-scale civil war, about which their counterparts in the west of the country had little knowledge.[6] On a different scale, the people of west Belfast may experience acute forms of violence, unfamiliar to rural communities in the region, and certainly unimaginable to most of Greater London's population.[7] Finally, it is difficult to assign a time-scale to this continuum. Many countries exhibit all the conditions and symptoms for an escalation into potential violent conflict, and yet continue for decades with no overt signs of conflict. Others may be stable and peaceful, but *appear* to erupt almost spontaneously.

From Civil Peace to Civil War

What causes a conflict to escalate? What triggers violence? And how can we assess whether a society is on the verge of violent conflict? In Figure 3.2 the interaction of a diverse range of political, social and economic factors which can contribute to the build-up of violence is presented. The use of such models provides a means of analysis and can help to give some early warning of impending violence.

Looking at the first column it is suggested that certain background or *systemic* factors such as bad colonial policies, cultural differences, resource scarcity, population growth, environmental degradation, unequal growth and poverty accentuate the possibilities for increased tension and conflict. But they are not in themselves sufficient indicators of where and when direct violence will emerge. Such

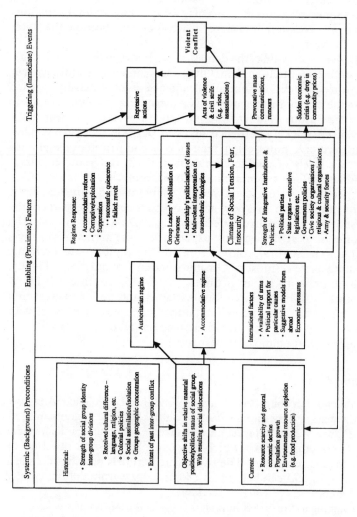

Figure 3.2 Sources of Violent Conflict[8]

factors permeate society, affecting large numbers of people, indirectly influencing and increasing the potential for overt conflict over long periods of time. Yet there may be no manifestations of physical conflict for years. Countries such as Indonesia, Egypt and India may exhibit many of the systemic symptoms which could lead to conflict: population growth, unequal wealth distribution and political repression (in the cases of Indonesia and Egypt). But occasional minor clashes and government clamp-downs notwithstanding, there have not been any other indications of *impending* communal violence. In other words, the writing may be on the wall, but it has been there so long that few people give it much credence.

Proximate[9] factors – that is, the government and the sociopolitical institutions which mediate between systemic factors and people's daily lives – are of immense importance in tackling conflicts of interest. If, for example, a state is accommodating to every cultural, religious or linguistic groups, then different identity groups feel no compulsion to assert themselves as a separate political entity. If there is democracy and freedom of the press, there are opportunities for people to air their grievances and call for political action. There may be profound economic problems, but there is no blanket suppression.

Yet if the poverty comes hand-in-hand with authoritarianism, corruption and repressive actions, the potential for conflict escalation rises. Often the state is so heavy-handed that for years no viable opposition can be formed. But because the state is violent in its actions, any opposition that does emerge, even if it begins peacefully, is often forced into a violent response. From Myanmar to Albania in March 1997 and perhaps Indonesia in the not so distant future, the descent into violence following years of repression is hardly surprising.

In many cases foreign intervention, be it through political support for a particular cause or repressive regime, economic pressures or sanctions or arms importation, can defuse or intensify a conflict. During the Cold War years, American support for military dictatorships helped quash popular opposition movements across Latin America. Similarly the Soviet Union's iron fist ensured there was no visible or viable dissent in Eastern Europe. Nowadays the situation is very different. Throughout Latin America and Eastern Europe, the pressure is on to democratise and liberalise. The stick that was military muscle has been replaced with the carrot that is financial incentive. But if governments do not regulate and ensure proper legislation and protection for their populations, there can be no guarantees of durable peace. Albania bears witness to that.[10]

The first bullets fired, the first tanks to roll in – these initial expressions of violence are the most *immediate* and *direct* causes of violent conflict. At this stage, a conflict has reached such a crisis

point that the slightest spark can cause an explosion. The threat
of pervasive and long-term violence increases as society enters a
cycle of economic decline, social fragmentation and a collapse of
law and order.

Sounding the Alarm – Devising a System for Early Warning

So what can be done to defuse tensions and stop the escalation of
conflict? That is the crux of the problem and one which any early
warning mechanism or system would aim to address. In other
words, the system should be able to identify the various factors which
provoke the intensification of conflict and specify actions which
could be taken at each stage to prevent the outbreak of further
violence. Discussions on the development of such a system address
three key areas.

1. Information gathering.
2. The analysis and understanding of that information.
3. Appropriate response.

Information Gathering

Access to information about particular countries or regions is
essential to any early warning mechanism. Information can be
gathered in a variety of ways by primary or secondary sources.
Primary sources can be classified as those present in the conflict
region, while secondary sources include institutions and academics
active in the qualitative and quantitative analysis of information.
These sources must be reliable and verifiable, the analysis must be
thorough and objective, and the information must be accessible and,
of course, timely. But at the heart of this debate lie the questions,
what type of information is needed?, and what can be deemed
relevant?

As discussed above, there may be a correlation between systemic
factors such as high neonatal mortality rates and violent conflict,
but it is neither sufficient proof nor necessarily the case that
countries with high neonatal mortality rates by definition experience
violent conflict. Alternatively, a focus on political structures alone
or even the extent of human rights abuses is not sufficient either.
For although such information may reveal the repressive nature of
the state, it gives little indication of the level of opposition or dissatisfaction amongst the population at large. Saudi Arabia is a case
in point. There is immense disparity in wealth, corruption is rife
at high levels and there is no political freedom, yet it is only in recent

months that the rumblings of dissent are being heard in the outside world. Given the West's interest in Saudi oil supplies, there seems little chance of a descent into outright war without concerted external attempts at conflict prevention.

The significance of historical animosities and latent conflicts cannot be overlooked, as the war in Bosnia illustrated only too clearly. However, age-old animosities and myths of battles lost and won *alone* do little to stir the public's conscience. A host of other conditions must also exist.

In general terms, the factors listed below can affect the gradation of conflict.

List 1: Factors Affecting the Gradation of Conflict[11]

- The intensity of grievances
- Parties' awareness of differences and separate identities
- Parties' perception and attitude towards each other
- Level of political mobilisation and organisation behind parties
- Extent of polarisation
- Amount of hostile behaviour
- Extent that parties use or threaten the use of arms
- Number of issues in dispute
- Number of parties supportive of each side
- Intensity of emotion and level of psychological investment in parties' positions and views of the world
- Amount of direct interaction and communication the parties have with one another
- Cohesion between leaders of respective parties and their constituencies

What kind of information *specifically* can help to measure these factors is more difficult to determine. For example, do sporadic racial attacks give a good indication of the intensity of grievances between parties? Is that a stronger indication than mutual public stereotyping and scaremongering? Or can the percentage of intergroup marriages give any indication of the degree of polarisation between groups? In other words, it is important to identify *essential conflict indicators* and establish a means of measuring and assessing changing conditions.

Another issue to consider is precisely who is involved in the information gathering process. To a large extent the quality and range of information available are determined by the collator. Perhaps more pertinently, the nature of the collator can affect and influence the interpretation of that information quite significantly. Listed below are just some of the sectors that can be involved.

Global and Regional Intergovernmental Organisations

The UN agencies, the OAU, the OSCE, ASEAN and the EU are just some of the intergovernmental organisations which have the mandate and resources to tackle security issues. With offices world-wide and a network of agencies working in the field of humanitarian relief, medical and environmental programmes, the UN is in a unique position to gather and disseminate information about potential conflicts from primary and secondary sources at all levels of the global political hierarchy. Some efforts were made in the past to create an early warning capacity for the organisation, including the short-lived Office of Research and Information (ORCI). The organisation also monitors a list of 'countries at risk', but this information is not publicly available. By virtue of having been established on the principle of state sovereignty and the non-interference in the internal affairs of states, the UN is limited in its ability to maintain public information regarding the level of risk or instability which any of its member states may be facing.

For example, the Algerian and Indonesian governments are doubtless unwilling to allow the UN to publicise its assessment of their domestic situation. To a great extent this is understandable, for if the UN were to declare that any country was 'at risk', there could be immeasurable damage to that country's economy and investments. This in turn could precipitate or lead to the escalation of a conflict situation.

Having said that, however, the Humanitarian Early Warning System (HEWS) does exist within the UN, and in the aftermath of Rwanda, the UN Department of Humanitarian Affairs has developed a global information system called ReliefWeb. Its purpose is to 'strengthen the response capacity of the humanitarian relief community through the timely dissemination of reliable information on prevention, preparedness and disaster response'.[12] It is not in itself an early warning *system*, and is limited in its direct contact with field operations and the regions being monitored. But by being accessible to the public, and providing regular updates and direct links to relevant information sources world-wide, it is definitely an added value tool which is enhancing information collection and management and access. Since its inception in October 1996, ReliefWeb has established information exchange systems with up to 170 humanitarian agencies world-wide and is now offering a multilingual service which provides daily updates on humanitarian emergencies and natural disasters. Future plans include a link into the Forum for Early Warning and Emergency Response (FEWER), a new early warning initiative which is discussed below.[13]

In recent years, the pertinence of early warning has been acknowledged by a number of organisations, and efforts are underway to establish information systems and databases. The creation of the post of High Commissioner on National Minorities at the Organisation for Security and Co-operation in Europe (OSCE) in particular reveals the increasing concern about intra-state conflicts. The High Commissioner has a specific mandate to intervene and attempt to prevent the outbreak of violence in internal disputes. The post was created as a response to the collapse of the USSR and the outbreak of a number of conflicts in that region. Since 1995, the High Commissioner has been actively involved in informal governmental consultations, offering recommendations for jurisdiction on the rights of minority groups throughout Eastern Europe and the former Soviet Union. The Centre for Conflict Prevention, based in Vienna, though still very small, is also concerned with co-ordinating short- and long-term OSCE missions. These include the monitoring of elections, peace agreements and troop movements in the region, and developing local capacities for early warning.

The Organisation of African Unity (OAU) has also taken steps towards recognising the need for co-ordinated information gathering and early warning mechanisms. To date, the OAU has initiated the development of a Conflict Prevention Centre, which aims to combine a data collection mechanism and an operations facility. However, according to a study concluded by the Netherlands Institute of International Relations (Clingendael) in 1996, such programmes are still in their infancy.[14] In examining the early warning and preventive actions of a number of intergovernmental organisations, the study reveals a lack of effectiveness and cohesion in their operations.

Finally, international financial institutions (IFIs) such as the World Bank and the IMF have access to useful information and are themselves instrumental in influencing the economies of many developing nations. The danger, however, is that strong economic indicators can be found even under the most oppressive regimes. So there may be very little information regarding the underlying socio-political conditions of the country. Recent efforts by the World Bank to address the problems of conflict have resulted in the creation of a new programme on post-conflict reconstruction.[15] Although early warning and early action are not specific foci of the programme, they are integral to the programme's success.

Individual Governments

Intelligence gathering has been a fundamental feature of state security for most governments. During the Cold War this feature was particularly heightened with the growth of organisations such as the CIA, KGB and MI6. These in turn were imitated by regimes throughout the world. However, with the demise of the single enemy, to a large extent the *raison d'être* of such intelligence agencies has also disappeared. Consequently many of the larger agencies have undergone a radical overhaul in recent years. Their operations have been significantly scaled down or withdrawn completely from certain regions. Of course, individual governments continue to receive information about their counterparts through diplomatic channels or where strong trade and political links exist. Thus they do have access to information regarding internal disputes and potential conflicts. Quite often, as in the case of France and Rwanda, strong historical links are manifested in military ties too. In such instances, the partner government is often highly aware of the internal political situation and of the potential levels of violence. Unfortunately, too often these relations are used to bolster regimes with armaments instead of encouraging negotiations and peaceful change.

There has been greater co-operation and information sharing through Interpol on drug trading, international criminal gangs and, most recently, terrorism. Although a number of governments may be keen to introduce more co-operative conflict information-sharing mechanisms, there is still a great deal of resistance to this idea, for it can impinge directly on the domestic and foreign political interests of each state.

NGOs, Humanitarian and Development Agencies

Countless international organisations exist with mandates to help the poor and starving in disaster-stricken areas, shelter refugees, campaign for the release of political prisoners, promote democratic values and assist in the physical development of nations. Their actions do benefit many people throughout the world and certainly create greater awareness in rich countries of the need to take action. In many instances, development and humanitarian agencies have access to the parties involved in a conflict. Often they have staff on the ground and local people involved in their long-term projects. Working at the grassroots level, they can detect signs of tension at an early stage, and are able to understand and assess the situation more accurately. Indeed, they may have knowledge of increases in violations of human rights or an impending attack. So their contributions to an international or regional information-gathering network can make an enormous difference.

Yet, they are restricted by their mandates in communicating this information with others as it is often regarded as a *breach of their neutrality.* Indeed, if they do breach their given mandates, they are at risk of expulsion. So although they can be an invaluable source of early warning information, they need to work within a wider international framework.

There are quite compelling strategic reasons for NGOs to develop their own early warning systems as opposed to relying on the UN or governments. First, advance knowledge can help in their forward and contingency planning and their own abilities to predict political upheaval and crisis. Thus, they can warn the population at risk of impending trouble and assist in ensuring their safety. Second, it can be critical in mounting effective advocacy campaigns and operational plans. Third, since governments are loath to admit to domestic problems, NGOs cannot simply rely on them for warning; nor can they rely on the UN with its current constraints. As a result, too often the cry for help comes when a situation has reached crisis point. Fourth, as is evident from ReliefWeb, the UN and governments themselves rely on NGOs as alternative sources of information. Finally, greater collaboration and co-ordination between NGOs could increase the efficacy of all their work. For if one human rights agency discovers an increase in the number of arrests in a region, that could be a sign of escalating social tensions and potential violence. By informing each other and alerting international bodies, their home governments and the international press and media, some early action could be taken.

In recent years, a number of the major agencies have initiated policies on early warning and early action. Amongst them, Amnesty International publishes an annual review of countries at risk. The Oxfam group of agencies also does a similar analysis, and shares it amongst the various satellite units. The Human Rights Documentation Exchange (HURIDOCS) is another international initiative engaged in developing bibliographic materials and developing standard formats for the recording of human rights violations. Over 400 NGOs participate in the collation and exchange of information.

Of course, the pitfalls and obstacles still need to be addressed. Ownership of information is a particular issue, for agencies are reluctant to act on the data of others; they prefer to source and use their own. There is also a lack of co-ordination between head offices, policy departments and field staff. In some cases there is hardly any co-ordination between various departments within the same organisation. Finally, despite numerous efforts and continuing work, developing a mutually acceptable and systematic protocol for data collection and analysis has proved very difficult. However, a number of region-specific networks have emerged to co-ordinate information. There is also a growing momentum for international NGOs to collaborate more closely in the future.

The Churches or Religious Communities

As a central feature of many societies, churches are amongst the first groups to detect significant changes in the socio-political environment. Religious groups have the ability to bring people together, rally support and take action. They can be involved in reporting human rights violations, speaking out against violence and promoting strong humanitarian and moral principles. Furthermore, with their wide international networks, religious organisations often have the best means of disseminating information into the international arena without jeopardising the lives of individuals on the ground.

Press and Media

The media, be it international, regional, national or local, television, radio, newspapers or the Internet, can play a pivotal role in providing early warning. On-line services such as Reuters or Associated Press, which have a network of reporters world-wide and a daily output accessible to all other sectors, are particularly useful in providing regular updates on events as they happen. A network of contacts with local journalists is also useful, as often they are witnesses to the escalation of tension and violence but are unable to publish reports in their own newspapers. Even journalists who arrive only at the critical point in a conflict can contribute to an early warning network.

However, the media, particularly the international mass media, are rarely interested in a conflict before it erupts. Moreover, television requires visually stimulating or shocking material, so the pre-conflict stage is rarely reported. Even when reporters are sent in, there is evidence to show that initial broadcasts often verge on sensationalism and can even be entirely inaccurate. This can cause immense confusion and encourage stereotyping, which in the long run does more harm than good. It is important that global news media such as CNN, Sky and the BBC World Service, while drawing attention to conflicts, also contribute towards resolving ambiguities and dispelling stereotypes rather than accentuating them. In this way, the media could be a powerful vehicle in galvanising public opinion and, by association, political action from world leaders.

Recent initiatives to incorporate journalism into early warning systems include the use of the Inter Press Service in mounting a conflict watch for African states. The growth of the Internet globally has also offered immense new opportunities for information sharing. The Zapatistas involved in the Chiapas conflict in Mexico, for example, are affiliated with a major web site, where a wealth of regularly updated information is available. In Albania, ordinary people are using web sites to voice their concerns about their country's future. Throughout the Bosnia conflict, people in Bosnia, Croatia and Serbia used e-mail to communicate with each other, thus bypassing state propaganda and censorship. However, there are still few monitoring mechanisms available, and just as the Internet could be used to initiate early warning or give marginalised and persecuted communities a global voice, it could also become a source of misinformation and propaganda.

The Academic Community

There are numerous research foundations and academic scholars researching and monitoring conflict areas. The academic community can make a valuable contribution to the theoretical discourse, regarding the nature of internal conflicts and reasons why some conflicts have escalated into violence, as in Yugoslavia, while others such as Malaysia and Canada have not. By analysing the raw data gathered by differing sources, and comparing contemporary situations with historic ones, they can shed light on the dynamics of conflict escalation. Furthermore, there is a wide range of active international academic networks through which information and experiences can be shared.

Amongst the more established research programmes is Ted Robert Gurr's Minorities at Risk programme, based at Maryland University. As mentioned in Chapter 2, by tracking and assessing a series of well-formulated indicators, this programme monitors the level of political and physical risk that ethno-political minority groups face within state boundaries. SIPRI, the University of Uppsala and PIOOM are three major European centres monitoring and studying potential crises situations, and ongoing armed conflicts. The work undertaken ranges from the monitoring of arms sales and movements to the death rates and levels of human rights violations in every country.

The Carnegie Commission on Preventing Deadly Conflict,[16] on the other hand, is a major research programme which, over a three-year period, has explored a wide range of issues relating to conflict, its prevention and resolution. Rather than focusing on specific indicators of conflict, the aim has been to broaden our general understanding of conflict, so that realistic recommendations for early action can be given to the UN, IGOs, the media, religious groups and other sectors of international and national society.

Civic Groups

Local community groups in the conflict region can become involved in monitoring the activities of the different sides in a conflict and provide key insights into the reasons for and motivation of each group. By virtue of being part of that society they have a more profound understanding of their compatriots. Thus they can play an immensely important role in providing information and analysing events.

Recent initiatives in regional conflict monitoring networks include the following:

1. In the former Soviet Union, the Institute of Ethnography and Anthropology has been at the centre of a vast network of contacts and information gatherers. The Kyrgyz Peace Research Centre, established in May 1996, is a network using six local monitors in the Ferghana Valley, a potential conflict region. In Tbilisi, Georgia, a network has been established by the Dutch INLIA to warn about refugee flows in the Caucasus. Information is supplied to the UNHCR.

2. The Emergencies Response Information Centre (ERIC) created by ACTIONAID in Kenya is an information and monitoring network for the Great Lakes region. Based in Nairobi, and operating on a 'go and see' basis, ERIC produces and disseminates monthly situation reports to an estimated 30 organisations.

3. Medgate, created at the Mediterranean Academy for Diplomatic Studies in Malta, is a joint venture between the North–South Centro of Lisbon and the Centre d'Informacio Internacionales of Barcelona. It is an Internet-based information exchange system which provides regular updates on social, economic, political and cultural issues in the Mediterranean region.

Although such initiatives are still in their infancy, they have the potential to make a significant impact on the way potential disputes are brought to the world's attention and managed at the national and international level.

For non-local organisations and agencies, the most efficient means of information-gathering is through regular fact-finding missions. Fact-finding is essentially conducting research in the field, talking and listening to local people, trying to understand their opinions, problems, fears, desires and needs, and making informed decisions based on those findings. All agencies – governmental, non-governmental, humanitarian and development – conduct regular fact-finding missions in the areas where they are active.

External fact-finding missions are important because they can play a neutral role in their assessment of the dynamics of a conflict by helping to map the fears and needs of peoples and communities at risk; identifying and analysing causal factors in conflict situations; promoting dialogue between parties to a conflict; generating alternatives to conflict; and channelling information and insights to potential actors working to mitigate or resolve particular conflicts. Other objectives include:

- bringing an international presence to bear on a situation;
- clarifying disputed facts;
- assisting international organisations in their deliberations on the conflict;
- bringing a process of dialogue between parties to a conflict;
- recording violations of accords or agreements;
- recording violations of human rights.

The use of databases as a means of collating information and giving greater accessibility to a wider audience is also important. They have the capacity to store detailed and historic materials which could be useful for analysis and understanding of a region. Yet, despite the existence of a wide range of databases world-wide, there is no single unit which compiles and analyses all the information with a particular focus on conflict prevention.

Some Existing Databases

1. Amnesty International: external country reports.
2. The Carter Center at Emory University in the United States.
3. The Farndon House Information Trust, UK: monitoring the sale of arms, publications in peace research.
4. Red Cross: disaster-related information.
5. One World On-line: an expanding database with links to a number of NGOs involved in global justice, conflict, aid, education, health, human rights and population.
6. SIPRI (the Swedish Peace Research Institute) lists countries at war, and monitors violence where there are over 1,000 deaths per year.
7. PIOOM (Dutch-based research institution) provides lists of countries at risk, involved in the development of standard formats, terminology and early warning indicators.
8. World Bank social development indicators.
9. Reuters: comprehensive world-wide news service.
10. United Nations: including GreenNet, UNHCR, ReliefWeb and HEWS.

11. Minorities at Risk group (University of Maryland) gathers empirical data on minority groups.

12. Institute of Ethnography in Russia has attempted to develop a computerised early warning system with a network of 40 local monitors across the former Soviet Union.

Information Analysis

Clearly, to a large extent, the information gatherers mentioned above undertake much of the analysis. However, given the limitations of each sector and the general level of mistrust, there is a basic lack of co-ordination amongst them. Fact-finding missions are often duplicated by a number of agencies and little is shared amongst the active parties. Governments and IGOs may have volumes of data, but without the resources to analyse and distil the information, nothing significant can be achieved.

The aim of analysis is to clarify how the information available can be used as an indicator of conflict escalation. In other words, a fact-finding mission undertaken in Rwanda in 1993 could have reported growing public unease and increasing ethnic tensions, but unless this information is assessed in relation to other socio-political issues, or compared to previous ethnic relations, then it gives little indication of the potential for conflict. A great deal of research is being undertaken to develop common sets of conflict indicators that could be applied world-wide.[17] For example, in Gurr's *State Failure Project* a total of 243 events were tracked over a 40-year period for numerous countries (see Table 3.1). Each event was described in a brief narrative report and given a score of between 1 and 4 in terms of its magnitude and seriousness. On the basis of this grading system and earlier empirical data, models were developed showing the various conditions which could lead to particular kinds of state failures: revolution, ethnic war, and so forth.

However, certain difficulties remain. At the most basic level, obtaining the necessary information from countries that are already in trouble is at times complicated or dangerous and may even be impossible.

At a more conceptual level, a gap remains between quantitative data analysis and more qualitative narrative-based reports. Quantitative analysis can be useful in monitoring and recognising the trends, particularly where figures of human rights violations are shown, but they have limited impact when political decisions need to be taken. Qualitative information, on the other hand, provides descriptive accounts of each event, but risks being perceived as too subjective. In part this problem is being tackled by combining indicator research with country case-studies. The latter provide a

Table 3.1 Possible Indicators for Early Warning[18]

Political and Leadership Issues	Criteria to be Measured
Regime capacity	Duration, democracy/ autocracy, revenue as share of gross domestic product
Characteristics of the elite	Ethnic and religious base, revolutionary leadership,exclusionary ideology
Political and economic cleavages	Extent and degree of group discrimination, group separation, income inequality
Conflictual political cultures	Revolution or ethnic war/genocide/ politicide, low level conflict in past 15 years
International influence	Military intervention, shifts in interstate conflict/ co-operation instability/ conflict in neighbouring countries

Economic and Environmental Issues	Level of pollution, impact on indigenous livelihood

Demographic and Societal Issues	
Population pressure	Density, total change in five years, youth bulge, cropland and labour force in agriculture
Ethnolinguistic diversity	Diversity, history of suppression
Militarisation of society	Military expenditure, five-year change in arms import, military v. medical personnel
Economic strength	level and change in per capita income and consumption
Quality of life	Access to safe drinking water, food supplies, infant mortality
Constraints on resource base	water depletion, soil degradation, famine
Government's economic management	Change in revenue and public sector debt, level of inflation, capital outflows, government reserves
Economic openness and trade	Import + export/GDP, direct foreign investment
International economic aid	Existence of IMF stand-by loan, other external aid

more in-depth and specific view of a particular crisis or country, but often such information is not transferable to other scenarios. However, by combining it with indicator data it is possible to extrapolate common key elements. In this way cross-country comparisons can be made without overlooking the unique features of each. Apart from developing indicators, work is also being undertaken to identify trigger mechanisms which lead to a dramatic escalation in the level of violence. A considerable amount of research is now underway to develop both quantative and qualitative data-sets for conflict situations.

Co-ordination between data collectors means that there must be an agreement on the terminology and the set of indicators used. So, for example, the term 'serious dispute' which is used by the UN cannot correlate with 'low-intensity conflict' as used by PIOOM, as the latter may have other meanings in UN definitions. This could cause much confusion and miscommunication. What is needed is a standardised reporting format to facilitate the exchange of information.

Responding Appropriately

But no matter how well planned a strategy may be, if no real action is taken to prevent the outbreak of violence, then any early warning information, case study, statistical data or sophisticated system of indicators is of little use. Rwanda bears witness to that.

From Early Warning to Mass Genocide – A Failure of Response[19]

In Rwanda, the UN and the NGO community were aware of heightening tensions long before the 1994 genocide took place. Between 1990 and 1994, civil violence against the Tutsi population gradually escalated. But observers linked the violence to the insurgency movements of the Rwandan Patriotic Front (RPF), a predominantly Tutsi army. Despite authoritative reports by the International Commission for Inquiry and the UN Commission on Human Rights on significant changes in the strategy of the Hutu extremists, and ominous signs of genocidal propaganda, little action was taken (even by UNHCR itself).

In the months preceding the genocide, extremist rhetoric filled the airwaves and characterised public rallies and even cocktail parties. Grave warnings of a planned coup, an assault on UN forces, provocation to resume the civil war and even detailed plans of genocidal killings in the capital reached the UN Secretariat in January 1994. The cable documenting this information was placed in a separate 'black file', designed to draw attention to its content and be circulated throughout the UN Secretariat. However, senior officials questioned its validity and made no contingency plans to avert the crisis. Similar reports to the French and Belgian governments were also ignored.

Within the UN there was no co-ordination of human rights violations with an analysis of the dynamics of social conflicts. At the time there were no links between information collection, analysis and the development of strategic policy options. One of the most significant sources of early warning, the UN human rights monitoring system was outside the Secretariat's information gathering network, and effectively become isolated from the decision-making process. In the field, the UN had no comprehensive or structured capacity for information collection. UNAMIR, the peacekeeping force, ran an irregular intelligence operation. The OAU had no capacity for data collection and analysis.

There was a failure to recognise the impending possibility of actual genocide, so much so that it was thought that the situation could be resolved within the confines of the UN, without recourse to the media spotlight. There was even verbal wrangling over the use of the word 'genocide'. Ultimately there was a general desensitisation to the situation, making the possibility of mass slaughter a reality.

Reasons for Failure – Lessons from Early Warning Systems

Rwanda proved that it was not necessarily the lack of *information* which hindered early action; rather, there were more critical and complex issues at stake.[20] In general terms, lessons learnt from the implementation and failure of early warning systems (EWS) for other crises, such as famine and natural disasters, offer useful insights. Quite clearly, sounding the alarm does not ensure any response, timely or otherwise. EWS are necessary, but they are not sufficient preconditions for the prevention of famine, conflict or refugee flows. Moreover, even where an EWS exists, reliance on one system can lead to trouble, for the focus may be on a region which generates much 'noise' or speculation, but where conditions are not the most severe. Given that resources and public and political attention are finite, it may be that the most critical situation receives no assistance.

Crisis Calibration

Another very important factor to emerge is that an effective early warning system must be carefully calibrated. Experience in famine situations has shown that while complex multi-indicators can identify a drought, the reference point for the EWS is actual famine. That is to say, action only comes when a famine has started, rather than in the months leading up to it when drought is occurring. People on the ground may know full well that the drought will lead to a famine, but assistance comes too late.

In the case of conflict early warning this calibration is also very important. Ideally the aim is to warn against the outbreak of mass violence before it becomes 'inevitable'. In essence, it is important to have different levels of warning depending on the gravity of the conflict situation. But deciding the optimal timing for such a warning can have significant implications for the government involved.

Co-ordination

Co-ordination (or its lack) between information gatherers, analysts, decision-makers and field-workers is still a major obstacle which needs to be tackled at many levels. First, amongst the international organisations including the UN and NGOs there is still a reluctance to share information or act on information gathered by others. Governmental and non-governmental groups cannot automatically trust every source, so unless the information comes from their own workers, or from a recognised, reliable source, little action will be taken. Furthermore, priorities may often differ, so while one is warning about an impending crisis in one region, another organisation is active in a different area and will not respond appropriately to the warnings. Even when there is a response, there may be conflicts of interest and little co-operation with field-based workers and community groups. Decision-makers and information analysts aim to maintain objectivity and in most circumstances cannot know what the most appropriate responses may be. Information gatherers and those experiencing the crisis are best placed to identify such responses, yet clearly their perspective is not entirely objective or even-handed with respect to other regions, which may also be suffering similar crises. As a result the action taken is often inadequate, of no benefit or in the worst cases actually serves to exacerbate a crisis.

Moreover, focusing on the capacities of northern NGOs and governments can mean that local strategies for identifying the indicators and responding to crises are overlooked. In addition, relief operations planned in London, New York or Geneva can neglect local problems such as the inadequacy of transport links, which can severely delay delivery. So aid in the form of seeds, for example, may be sent, but by the time it reaches the crisis region it may be too late for sowing. This issue is particularly pertinent to conflict EW. For it is self-evident that early warning information disseminated amongst external actors and governments will not ease the tensions and conflict which exist in a country. Without communication and the partnering of *external* and *internal* capabilities, an EWS is of little consequence.

Intelligence v. Early Warning

Most governments will rarely regard mounting tension in another state as a priority. Consequently action is taken only when conflict has broken out and refugees are on the move. Furthermore, confusion and suspicion can arise between the purpose and functions of an early warning system versus that of an intelligence system. Intelligence gathering is cloaked in secrecy. Particularly within undemocratic regimes, it is viewed with great suspicion and seen as a covert and informal means of identifying signs of organised resistance or grassroots dissatisfaction. Early warning, on the other hand, seeks to be transparent, and in so being makes the information accessible to a wide audience. It should be public information, drawn from the public sources.

Information v. Analysis

Another difficulty faced by governments is the ratio of raw information available to the degree and quality of analysis which it undergoes, and the range of concrete recommendations for action that are made. Furthermore, since government departments have different priorities and agendas, even if recommendations are made in one department, it is unlikely that they are adhered to in another, or indeed by political leaders. So traditionally there has been very little integration between relief, development, foreign and military policies.

Political Will

Even where there is policy coherence, decision-makers tend to demand hard evidence of a crisis. In other words, reports of the disappearance or slaughter of refugees and predictions of attacks are not enough to trigger the process of providing aid and other assistance. Not surprisingly, by the time the 'hard' evidence (pictures, film footage, direct diplomatic accounts) is available, it is too late for warnings or preventive action. Of course, the lack of accountability on the part of a donor government has a direct influence on their inaction. Donors, particularly donor governments, are not accountable to those whom they assist. But they are accountable to varying degrees to their public at home and to the media for short periods of time. So there are no real, long-term incentives or pressures to motivate richer governments to help.

Furthermore, it would be naive to assume that governments actually want to intervene or assist in political crises. The truth is that in most cases they prefer not to know in advance, because then there would be pressure and a sense of obligation to take action. Too often, they are not sure of the action that could or should be taken. In other words, there is a fundamental lack of political will to take early preventive action. This is further compounded by a lack of strategy and of relevant and effective 'instruments' for intervention.

Despite these logistical and structural difficulties, it is a sobering thought that in the case of Rwanda, it was neither a lack of co-ordination between the UN and NGOs, nor a lack of concrete evidence about the scale of the genocide which stalled the UN. For once it seemed that all field reports pointed to the same impending crisis. The UN even had its own forces stationed there. Numerous NGOs were running development programmes across the country. The warnings were going through to the UN headquarters in New York and to the Secretary General's own office. The fact was that Rwanda was not a priority for Security Council members. Only France had a foothold, and her sympathies were predominantly towards the Hutus, not the threatened Tutsis. Given its history of communal violence, the threat of conflict was nothing new. More pertinently, Rwanda had little strategic value or valuable natural resources such as oil. In contrast to the Gulf War for which all international standards and conventions were invoked through the United Nations, Rwanda was deemed of such little consequence that not even the 'Genocide Convention' was agreed upon. Moreover, the Somalian experience ensured that no western power (particularly the US) would risk more 'body bags' coming home from inexplicable conflicts in far-away places in the name of humanitarianism. The mass killings of a million people did nothing to change that attitude.

Generating Early Action

So we return to the question, what can be done to generate early action and overcome political reluctance?

In part better co-operation and co-ordination of the activities of various parties could improve early responses. If, for example, one agency has a strong ground staff and networks with local groups in country A, but only desk officers in country B, while another agency is weak in country A and strong in B, the ground staff of the former can contribute to the information gathering in A, while the second agency contributes to the data analysis. In contrast, in country B, the second agency can provide raw data while the first does the analysis. This analysis could then be forwarded to relevant IGOs and governments to assist in their policy-and decision-making processes, thereby avoiding the sensitive issue of IGOs 'spying' on their member states.

The other part relates to the willingness of intergovernmental organisations and individual governments to co-operate and support NGOs. There will always be differences in opinion and attitude. Still, governments and IGOs are beginning to appreciate the comparative advantages of working with NGOs as they tend to be committed to long-term action, are willing to invest time and resources in specific issues, and have a wealth of grassroots experience and expertise. On humanitarian emergencies, for example, the UNSC meets with a joint committee of NGO representatives. Similar initiatives are being taken in Africa where a consultative council of NGOs holds meetings with the OAU's Council of Foreign Ministers to discuss conflict regions. Another effective development has been the monthly gathering of the Central Africa Great Lakes Forum in Washington. Representatives from the State Department, the diplomatic corps, media, specialists and NGOs come together to exchange information and discuss policies regarding international action in the region. These coalitions can also mount effective advocacy campaigns to generate public interest and political will.

NGOs do need to be realistic about government attitudes. Most elected governments do not look beyond the next election, so they aim to make maximum impact in the shortest possible time. In other words, it is preferable for them to intervene and offer assistance in an existing crisis rather than aim to prevent the outbreak of another in ten years' time. Still, NGOs can be most effective if they complement and augment the UN and bilateral governmental activities. In isolation they do not have the political, economic or military options which could be brought into play to encourage states to co-operate. The key, therefore, is to ensure cross-sectoral co-ordination and a division of labour based on the comparative advantages of each. In this way political interest can be built up over time, making it more likely for the necessary action to be taken at particular times.

Already amongst members of the Organisation for Economic Co-operation and Development (OECD), the need for a division of labour and co-operation between donor countries and embassies within the region of conflict as part of an early warning system is increasingly being acknowledged.[21] It is argued that with regular communication between these parties, a *common base of information* about a conflict could be agreed upon. This information could then be used to formulate a co-ordinated strategy, recognised by all

OECD members, while being sensitive to the needs of the various disputing factions.

Presentation of Information

Another criterion for generating early action relates to the presentation of early warning information to key policy- and decision-makers. In other words, the provision of reams of statistical data or long qualitative reports is not the most effective means of 'grabbing attention'. Instead, information gatherers and EW advocates need to be more 'response- oriented'.[22] In other words, they should target their analyses so that they are easy to understand and easy to use by policy end-users. This would involve taking four key questions into consideration at the earliest stages. First, what and who are the actors responsible for acting on EW analysis, and what is their capacity? Second, what are the policy frameworks and bureaucratic mandates by which decisions are made? Third, what are the corresponding resource constraints and operational frameworks? Fourth, what is the most efficient and effective means of disseminating EW information?

In terms of information analysis, it is important to highlight *patterns* and trends of relative deprivation or discrimination. The array of indicators must be fused together and graded according to importance thus providing a fully integrated and dynamic picture of events. In other words, reports of urban rioting in Kenya alone may be ignored by other governments, but those reports, coupled with a focused analysis of the socio-political state of the country, the growing levels of human rights abuses and increasing arms flows, give an ominous and worrying indication of an imminent outbreak of conflict.

The grading and highlighting of the most critical conflict factors are important, since they can be targeted for operational responses and can be matched to the policy frameworks of the various actors and organisations involved. In other words, if, as in the case of Kenya, constitutional issues are at the heart of the conflict, it could be that the Commonwealth Secretariat offers its diplomatic and political assistance to reassess and even help redraft the constitution in conjunction with the disputing parties. At the same time, if election monitors and observers are requested, the UN and NGOs could step in. Finally, as is often the case, if the government in question is unwilling to seek this assistance or invite the monitors willingly, informal bilateral diplomacy could be utilised to encourage openness and compromise. In this way, immediate tensions could be diffused, while the initial source of conflict could also be addressed.

In an attempt to address these wide and disparate issues and bridge the gap between information gatherers, policy-makers, external and internal actors, the FEWER (Forum for Early Warning and Emergency Response) project has been developed by a consortium of NGOs, IGO representatives and UN agencies.

The FEWER Project[23]

The Forum for Early Warning and Emergency Response (FEWER) is a multidisciplinary consortium of approximately 20 international NGOs and UN agencies and governments involved in conflict research, campaigning and developmental issues. *The objective of FEWER is to develop a single coherent system of conflict indicators, reporting and, most significantly analysis and policy recommendations, which could assist and influence policy-makers in their decisions.*

Standard formatting of reports, a common terminology and an agreed list of indicators are being developed to ensure coherence and uniformity. Working closely with UN agencies and the EU is a means of ensuring communication and co-operation on policy planning, development and implementation. It is also an effective means of exposing NGOs to the policy frameworks and constraints within which IGOs function.

Although this network is still at an early stage of development, it is hoped that by creating a regular forum for communication between different types of NGOs and UN agencies, there will be a greater exchange of information, greater trust and a general increase in awareness regarding the complex and wide-ranging factors which can impact conflicts.

Initially three regions will be focused on. To avoid confusion and duplication, three lead agencies, each corresponding to a region, will be selected. Their task is to gather, sort and analyse the plethora of information that emerges about each region from their partner agencies and other sources.

The governments of Sweden, Canada and Holland, the European Commission and European Parliament support FEWER. A further 14 IGOs are also involved, including UNDHA, UNHCR and UNICEF.

Taking Action

Assuming that awareness and concern for potential conflict exist and the political will is sufficiently generated to call for action, the question which arises next is, what sort of action could realistically be taken? What strategies could be developed by the international community, governments or local communities? The events of 1996–97 in the Democratic Republic of Congo (formerly Zaire) reveal the complexity of each situation.

Genocide Revisited – The Killing Fields of Zaire[24]

From inside the huge C-130 ... cargo planes ... it's easy to see how 220,000 people could just disappear in this country's interior. Below, as far as the eye can see in every direction is jungle ... Mere grass is eight feet tall ... Forbidding terrain is helping to perpetuate this cycle of genocide. It is cloaking the work of the killers and hiding the victims from the eyes of the world.[25]

It was common knowledge amongst UN staff, aid workers, the media and governments that a fair number of *genocidaires*, and extremist Hutu militias who had mounted the Tutsi genocide in 1994 were living amongst the 1.2 million Rwandan Hutus in the refugee camps of eastern Zaire. But it was also well known that the large majority of refugees were innocent civilians, who fled the advances of the Tutsi-led army in the summer of 1994. For two years they lived in the camps, trying to bring a semblance of normality to their lives. Then, in September 1996, as Laurent Kabila's forces with assistance from the Tutsi-dominated Rwandan army advanced, the camps came under attack.

Fearing mass killings, international aid workers and observers in the area called for military intervention to protect the refugees, but by November 1996, television images were portraying rivers of people, with music and dance, making their way home to Rwanda. The NGO community was criticised for 'crying wolf', and the Canadian government which had spearheaded a move to send in troops was embarrassed internationally as the Rwandan government was seen to welcome home its people.

Yet, the plight of an estimated 220,000 people who had fled into the jungle interiors was still unknown. By virtue of not returning home they were assumed 'guilty' and, according to numerous reports, hunted down and killed. Stories of mass killings, machete attacks and systematic executions were denied by Kabila and the Rwandese. The international community demanded 'hard evidence', but no one was permitted into the vast area. No inspections were carried out and no witnesses came forth willingly. But by June 1997, evidence, first-hand tales and witnesses began to filter through. Those who survived the ordeal of disease and death have emerged to tell their stories. Soldiers with orders to kill and burn bodies and local villagers forced to help in digging graves and burying bodies are speaking out. Revenge and retribution: the cycle of violence continues on.

It could be argued that the international community did make a concerted effort to protect the Rwandan refugees in Congo, but were hampered by a combination of local political issues and significant practical issues. The region is vast and the terrain inhospitable; once the refugees had dispersed it was almost impossible to bring them back. The question, however, is whether the international community could have averted this tragedy from the outset. Given that it was well known that the camps harboured the guilty alongside the innocent, that the former still controlled the majority of the population and that elements within the Tutsi-dominated Rwandan army were bound to seek revenge, could not the UN and major donor governments have developed a strategy to disarm the militias and give protection to the innocent? Could there not have been a plan to seal and close off the Rwandese and Burundian borders to Zaire, and so thwart both Tutsi and Hutu militia attacks on civilians? The situation was complex and opinions varied in every quarter. But in the final analysis, the refugees were not afforded basic protection.

A Range of Options

Every conflict is unique, so there can never be a rigid set of rules or strategies to follow. According to the stage of conflict and the intensity of violence, however, certain criteria can be taken into consideration, (see Table 3.2 for a selection of options).[26] For example, taking the peace–war continuum in relation to time (see Figure 3.3),[27] if there is a general awareness that tensions and discrimination exist between particular ethnic groups within a *stable* society, medium to long-term strategies could be designed to break down the barriers and improve communication and understanding between them. Employment policies, educational opportunities, community networks and joint economic programmes could be developed to establish links and create a mutually reliant and beneficial relationship. In Malaysia, following rioting by the minority Chinese population in the 1960s, a new political policy was implemented to give the Chinese better access to education and economic and political opportunities. The result has been that although the Chinese have less access to and control of the political arena, they are more dominant in the world of trade and business than their Malay counterparts. Thus there is a degree of mutually acceptable parity.

If, however, tensions have increased, the political situation is *unstable* or a state of emergency has been declared, the government's legitimacy is questioned and violent confrontation seems likely, then *conflict prevention* mechanisms could be applied. First and foremost the dispute must be acknowledged and parties should engage in dialogue. External diplomatic assistance can come in the form of 'good offices', informal consultation and conciliation efforts, or even in the form of public condemnation to press the state to conform to international standards.

International troops can be deployed, as in the case of Macedonia in 1994–95, to maintain peace, while diplomatic efforts encourage dialogue between the disputants. In the Baltic states, for example, mediation between minority Russians and the majority nationalist groups has continued discreetly over a number of years. With the help of retired western military personnel, sensitive issues such as defence and security, the role of military and the underlying fear of attack from Russia have been greatly allayed.

Local and community-based conflict resolution mechanisms could be supported and mediation attempts made. If there is a threat of armed action or military reprisal, action could be taken to build the public's confidence in the military. Mass media could be encouraged to promote communication and understanding through objective and in-depth reporting.

The objective at this stage is to foster communication between disputants and discourage extremist action. The strengthening of civil and political institutions is also important, as is attempting to alleviate the most desperate factors which are breeding frustration and conflict. At this early stage social and political ties exist and disputants have yet to become polarised or extreme in their views.

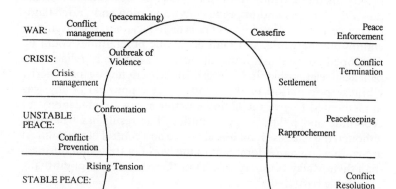

Figure 3.3 Stages of Intervention along the Peace–War Continuum

There is greater flexibility on all sides to accept a process of negotiations and compromise. Furthermore, so long as the guns lie untouched and there are no deaths, the sense of injustice, hurt, fear and hatred is limited, so the chances of resolving the conflict non-violently are still good.

If the tensions are not alleviated and concrete efforts are not made to resolve the conflict, the situation can reach a point of *crisis*. At this stage a series of short- and medium-term strategies should be implemented. The objective in such situations would be to reduce tensions and prevent violence in the short term, while creating other avenues for tackling the sources of the dispute in the medium to long term. Official diplomatic activities could range from coercive measures and sanctions, to the provision of good offices for mediation and negotiations. External peacekeeping forces could be called in, in parallel with grassroots conflict resolution mechanisms and conditional economic assistance. As in Kenya during 1997, local communities, NGOs and civil society could press for political institution-building, the monitoring of human rights violations, elections and power-sharing arrangements.

By the time war breaks out, the level of communication between disputants has sunk so low that, in part, an intervention would have to focus on recreating the space for discussion, while pressing for a ceasefire. At times it is possible to 'manage' a conflict by finding areas for co-operation between political leaders. However, this can only be sustained if real measures towards resolution are introduced and accepted. In Burundi, for example, throughout 1995 a UN initiative to form a coalition government of Hutus and Tutsis was partly successful in reducing the intensity of violence. It was rejected, however, by extremist opposition groups, who moved to Zaire and launched regular attacks against civilians and politicians. The coalition finally broke down. The violence, from all sides, has subsequently been relentless.

Often internal wars continue for years, through cyclical periods of increasing and decreasing violence. Opportunities for peacemaking may come regularly, but just as regularly efforts are thwarted. In Sri Lanka, throughout the decade or so of war, a myriad of peace initiatives have come and gone, but at every point each side becomes even more intransigent and determined to fight to the bitter end.

Still, a range of external and internal efforts can be considered. The most obvious external interventions usually come at the height of tension or violence. It can be shuttle diplomacy, as with former President Carter visiting Haiti one weekend and Bosnia the next; or even a straight military attack as in NATO's dramatic bombardment of Serb positions in 1995 after four years of international inertia. Sanctions, arms embargoes and humanitarian assistance could also be implemented. In the midst of violence, the

Table 3.2 A Matrix of Conflict Prevention Tools[28]

Human Rights	Communication and Education	Military Measures	Economic and Social Development
• Mediation • Negotiation • Conciliation • Informal consultation • Peace conference • Unilateral goodwill gestures • Civilian fact-finding missions • Observers/ Monitoring/ Verification teams • Special envoys • Conflict prevention/ management centres • Human rights monitoring • Promotion/ advocacy of HR standards • HR institution-building	• Support local conflict management/ resolution • Conflict management/ resolution training • Peace commissions • Non-official facilitation/ Problem-solving workshops • Civilian peace monitors • Internationally sponsored peace consultations • Exchange visits • Conflict resolution/ prevention centres • Peace education • Visits by eminent organisations/ individuals (embarrassing witnesses) • 'Friends' groups • Non-violent campaigns	• Pre-emptive peacekeeping forces • Professionalise/ restructure military forces • Demobilisation/ reintegration • Military to military programmes • Military confidence building and security measures • Non-aggression agreements • Security guarantees • Targeted deterrence • Demilitarised zones • Arms embargo/ blockades • Threat/projection of force • Crisis management • Arms-proliferation control • Alternative defences	• Targeted economic assistance • Economic reform • Economic cooperation/ integration • Inter-communal trade • Private economic investment • Health assistance • Agricultural programmes • Conditionality for conflict prevention • Environment/ natural resource management

Judicial/Legal Processes and Arrangements	Media/Journalism	Humanitarian Assistance	Political Development Governance
• Commissions of enquiry/war crimes tribunals • Constitutional commissions • Judicial/legal reforms • Police reform • Support local indigenous legal institutions • Arbitration • Adjudication	• Peace Radio/TV • Joint investigative reporting projects • Media profes-sionalisation • International journalist training • Civic education • Formal education projects • Peace education	• Humanitarian aid • Repatriation/resettlement of refugees • Capacity building for public welfare	• Political institution building • Election monitoring • National conferences • Capacity building of civil society • Power-sharing arrangement • Sub-national devolution and autonomy • Capacity building of authorities/training public servants

tools used must have immediate impact. But such 'strong arm' tactics must go hand-in-hand with the offer of negotiations, conditional economic assistance, the opportunity of justice and reform, and the long- to medium-term measures mentioned above are needed for peace to have any chance.

If outside intervention does come, it may be in the form of peace enforcement as in Bosnia, or unofficial private dialogue as in Northern Ireland. It is perhaps the most intractable period of a conflict, for attitudes have hardened, there is a profound sense of hurt and injustice on all sides, and often the disputants have become fragmented and disparate. But at the same time, people have grown weary of fighting and are disillusioned, so there are opportunities for encouraging ceasefires and a return to the negotiation table.

Agreement to a ceasefire, mutual agreement to talk and draw up peace settlements – at this point of 'conflict termination', the critical issue of direct violence is brought to an end. But it is just one small battle that has been won, not the entire war. Insecurities are rife, tensions are still high and the chance of failure is greater than that of success. Yet given the right conditions and participation of key actors, the signing of a peace declaration can be the first step towards sustainable peace. In Mozambique, for example, after three decades of war, peace has finally begun to take hold. Intervention may come in the form of UN peacekeeping troops or monitors, ensuring that no agreements are violated. It may also come in the form of local and regional parties who drive the peace process forward with public support. Whatever its manifestations, it is the beginning of much longer-term reconciliation and post-conflict peace-building work.

Sceptics and Critics

Before concluding this chapter it is important to acknowledge the various arguments countering the concepts of early warning and early action. For certainly there are the cynics who think that such ideas are completely delusional.[29] Sitting comfortably in London or New York and contemplating the ways and means in which the tragedies of Bosnia, Somalia or Rwanda could have been averted, is, they argue, a purely theoretical exercise. Prevention may be feasible with the benefit of hindsight, but not at the moment it is needed. No amount of analysis or experience can account for unpredictable factors, be they the spontaneous actions of individuals, the accidental pull on a trigger or the reckless commands of a despot. Besides, given that no two conflicts are ever the same, any experience and information gained in one situation can never be a 'design' or blueprint for effective intervention in another.

Even if a plausible course of preventive action could be determined, mustering the necessary resources and the public and political support to implement it would, they argue, be a near-Herculean task. Prevention of any sort has to be justified against the risk of potential damage and cost. Even in the medical world, preventive medicine is easily targeted, for it is difficult to determine the true cost of accidents or epidemics that have not yet occurred. In the world of global politics where those who bear the costs are not themselves the beneficiaries of the action, preventive action is faced with an even greater challenge. In other words, the political will needed to take action is grounded in political realities and necessities. Moreover, since there can be no systematic means of analysing and evaluating the financial value or the effectiveness of the action taken, there are no persuasive 'before' and 'after' arguments that can be made. In other words, it is all but impossible to prove that a 'war' that never happened has been prevented. Furthermore, too much preventive activism, that is, early warnings, followed by costly preparations but no outbreak of conflict can also deter governments. Often it is the combination of actions from various sources that helps deter conflict escalation. Consequently it is very difficult to give credit and justification for each individual act. So the likely conclusion on the part of many governments will be that their preparations are unnecessary, and that the activists are merely 'crying wolf'.

Advocates of this form of 'delusion theory' argue that given the increasing parochialism and short-term vision of powerful governments, a policy of long-term conflict prevention, which is difficult to evaluate and brings no glory, is hardly a credible candidate for international activism. Selling the concept of conflict prevention to a democratic government is, they say, like trying to sell a pension policy to a teenager: they are simply not interested in paying now in the hope of reaping the rewards in the long and uncertain future. All in all, therefore, conflict prevention is idealism, a waste of resources and quite simply a delusion.

Intervention as Perversion

Beyond the 'delusionists' come the supporters of the 'perversion' theory. They go even further, arguing that not only does prevention not work, but it is likely to exacerbate potential conflict situations. On the one hand, intervention in a conflict about which little is understood can have unintended consequences. It can even bring about that which it aimed to prevent. In other words, any action, despite its good intentions, can backfire. On the other hand, predicting a conflict can become a self-fulfilling prophecy. Fear can generate more fear, and tensions may rise needlessly. Finally and contrarily, it is important to realise that in many cases the majority populations who are living under difficult and tense circumstances often do not want to admit that violence is impending. Even when from the outside a society may appear to be on the brink of war or violence, those within do not want to accept the reality of their situation. In Bosnia, Chechnya and Rwanda, time and again, ordinary civilians were stunned by the events that took place. They were unprepared for the onslaught of terror and had no means of countering the propaganda and actions instigated by the more extremist factions of their society.

Furthermore, in unstable and volatile conditions, warnings can sound like provocation or incitement to take action. The warnings of one side can be manipulated into the propaganda of their adversaries. Some parties may feel even more threatened and marginalised. Any warning of impending violence can result in the sudden flight of thousands, or pre-emptive retaliation, before other solutions have been attempted. Preventive action can also be interpreted as favouring one side over the others, thereby escalating tensions even further. In particular, the involvement of NGOs is questioned. Deemed to be 'loose cannons', and accountable to no other authorities, NGOs are accused of siding with particular groups, hindering governmental peacemaking efforts and, as a result, of damaging the entire process.

Another dimension of the 'perversion' theory is that short-term successes gained through early action can become long-term failures. Not all sides benefit from the early diffusion of conflict, so what may appear to be the resolution of a conflict is in fact a state of 'suspended conflict', which could flare up at a later stage. More simply, the argument implies that some conflicts are necessary and inevitable for long-term social and political change; that it is often necessary for grievances to be voiced and for conflicts to intensify before they are resolved. The challenge, they say, is to contain the intensity of violence, and to intervene when both sides have run their course and the conflict is 'ripe'. Even then, the potentially negative effects of intervention can be tremendous deterrents for many states. Often, states that are a party, or potential party, to a conflict regard the involvement of external actors as a direct challenge to their sovereign rights and powers. For those external actors, especially if they are states, the simple act of showing interest or taking steps to prevent a conflict at an early stage locks them into the conflict and raises their stakes and incentives for its resolution. In other words, if the United States or France takes an active interest in Burundi, the failure to resolve the situation reflects badly on them as external intervenors as well.

Prevention as Diversion

The next set of arguments comes under the banner of the 'diversion' theory, which questions the effectiveness of prevention. The prevention of violent conflict is a fascinating and even alluring notion, but its implementation would be detrimental to the existing network of international structures and relations. Government involvement in the internal affairs of other states could ultimately result in a desta-bilisation of inter-state relations. Furthermore, the resources and funds spent on conflict prevention could be put to better use elsewhere. Critics of the UN are already complaining about the increased costs of security and peacekeeping operations. To give it greater priority would be to reduce or shift expenditure in the field of economic and social development. So, for example, development projects with a slant on conflict prevention could be favoured over other projects. Countries at greater risk of conflict would be prioritised over those which are equally needy, but more stable. Yet given that there are no guarantees that prevention measures could actually work, there is a danger of wasting resources and depriving other countries of a chance for stable development as well. Quite simply, the arguments imply that given the wide spectrum of worthy causes and the limited resources available, the opportunity costs of conflict prevention are too high to make it a viable course of action.

Conclusion

These arguments are certainly persuasive and must be taken heed of, but they still do not provide a viable answer to the problems and dangers that the world currently faces. The fact is that intra-state conflicts are increasingly prevalent, and the existing global institutions are not sufficiently equipped to prevent or resolve them. In essence, the arguments in favour of early warning and early action advocate that if the potential for violent internal conflict is acknowledged, a series of complementary approaches and tools could be implemented across different socio-political sectors to quell the tensions and dispel high levels of violence. They do not advocate the suppression of change or transformation.

To a great extent, the tools and approaches outlined in this chapter have grown out of existing official diplomatic channels which are attuned to the prevention of *international* conflicts. In the following chapter, the development of these diplomatic processes are examined. We also discuss ways in which the system of inter-national diplomacy and inter-state relations could be expanded to benefit from the growth of citizen-based activities in situations of internal conflicts.

CHAPTER 4

The Diplomacy Continuum

A famous surgeon was asked if his fame came from being the best doctor in the village. The man replied, 'I have an elder brother who can see an illness coming and stops it before it takes hold of a person's body. Yet because he stops the illness before it spreads, no one has ever heard of him. I also have a second brother who can prescribe medication before illness ravages a patient's body. He is known by those he has saved, but not by others. And I come last, for my skill is in removing the disease from the ravaged body. I am called when the disease has spread beyond control. Yet I am more famous than my brothers, for it is then that people understand how dreadful a disease can really be.'

(from an old Japanese fairytale)

Introduction

'An ambassador', said Sir Henry Wotton during his time as ambassador and diplomat in the court of King James I, 'is an honest man sent to lie abroad for the good of his country.'[1] Centuries later his compatriot and fellow diplomat, Geoffrey McDermott, offered a less cynical but still revealing definition of his profession.

> Diplomacy is concerned with the management of international relations. Every state, whatever its calibre and size, wants to maintain or improve its position in the world. That is a fact; though it is also a fact that the world would be better off with far fewer nationally-minded states.[2]

No doubt the cynicism is well founded, but it is also true that at its very core the practice of diplomacy is about the avoidance of outright violence in the midst of competition and conflicts of interest. In other words, good diplomatic practice is about seeking alternative avenues of dispute resolution and compromise, so as to ensure consensus amongst all parties. In effect, the practices and structures of international diplomacy are themselves the tools of early warning and early preventive action in relation to inter-state conflicts.

However, as Chapter 3 has illustrated, existing state-based structures have not always proved successful in preventing intra-state conflicts, so there is a need to explore fresh approaches and new developments in the field of conflict prevention. From the early days of imperial emissaries, through to the formation of embassies and recognised conventions of diplomatic practice, until now, where through a multitude of socio-economic, political, medical, military and technological developments ever-greater numbers of people are linked together globally, inter-state diplomatic relations have expanded and changed. In every field, including peacemaking, citizen groups and non-governmental organisations are able to complement the work of official structures. We begin, therefore, by suggesting that the acceptance and inclusion of such avenues for dialogue in peacemaking are a natural development within a dynamic continuum of diplomatic practice.

Traditional Diplomacy Through the Ages

The general characteristics of modern diplomacy can be traced through history and human civilisation. In part defined as 'tact, skill and cunning in dealing with people', the practice of diplomacy undoubtedly dates back to humanity's early days. As is often pointed out, early diplomacy must have developed when human societies decided and agreed that it was better to hear the message than to eat the messenger.[3] Thus emerged the first tenet of diplomacy: the principle of diplomatic immunity. The acceptance of this principle even amongst normally warring empires is evidenced in the fifth century BC when the Persian king Darius sent emissaries under the flag of truce to every Greek state, demanding the symbolic 'earth and water' from each. The Spartans' and Athenians' blunt rejection of this peace offensive – they executed the emissaries – was regarded as breaking the bonds of civilised negotiations and an invitation to war.[4]

Diplomacy of one form or another was widely practised amongst the empires of China, Egypt, Persia, India, Greece and Rome. Its purpose was wide-ranging and varied, encompassing matters of state, the military and trade. By about the second century BC, the trans-Asian silk road, which connected China to India, the Middle East, Rome and Alexandria, had led to significant contact between disparate cultures. Buddhism had already spread from India to China, and records suggest that a number of maritime embassies from Rome and Syria existed in China.

The term *diplomacy* is derived from the Greek word 'diploma', which refers to the official state document or certificate which not only gave the bearer, the '*diplomat*', certain privileges such as diplomatic immunity as his nation's official representative, but also authenticated him in the eyes of other governments and neighbouring city states. In the modern context, diplomacy can be defined as 'the art or practice of conducting *international* relations, as in negotiating alliances, treaties, and agreements'.[5] Intrinsic to the term *international* (between nations) is the acceptance of the nation-state as the central actor in political and diplomatic affairs.

From a modern *western* standpoint, ancient Greece offers the first elaborate models of state diplomacy for which there is a wealth of evidence.[6] Unlike the hierarchical system of governance that existed in other empires, the Greeks' combination of small, equally powerful city-states called for a system that would allow them to communicate as *equals*. Different types of envoys and emissaries were sent depending on the gravity or nature of the mission. The range of words referring to 'reconciliation', 'temporary local truce', 'convention', an 'alliance', 'commercial treaty' and the 'conclusion of peace' also reveals the elaborate system of diplomatic communication that existed. Furthermore, the Olympic Games and other festivals during which a solemn and sacred truce was declared, so that arrangements could be made in a spirit of co-operation, are perhaps the earliest forms of international organisations.

In Byzantium, diplomacy became more sophisticated and played a larger part in political negotiations. For the first time, government departments wholly concerned with external affairs and foreign negotiators were established. The basis of diplomatic protocol, pomp and ceremony was heightened, and no opportunity was lost to impress visiting allies and potential enemies with displays of the empire's military strength and its divine, mystical powers. The Byzantines' own ambassadors were trained in the art of negotiation, given written instructions and told to be courteous, praising and never critical of their foreign hosts.

The idea of placing the empire or state above all else became a formidable basis upon which diplomatic negotiations took place, allowing them to work slowly and patiently. Flattery, general duplicity and, most significantly, bribery in foreign relations was justified in the name of the empire. Huge payments to local potentates and chieftains were regarded as a sound investment and an effective preventive measure against a rebellion or war. When the coffers ran low, the most ancient of tactics, strategic marriage, was used to cement relationships.

Renaissance Italy, with its intricate system of small states each fighting for territory, power and ultimately survival, led to further developments in the diplomatic sphere. Whereas in the past envoys and emissaries were sent on an ad hoc basis, in the fifteenth century a new breed of permanent diplomats with official foreign postings emerged and later spread throughout Europe. Diplomacy became a game of high stakes, combining ruthless cunning with recklessness. Stratagem, opportunism, deception, suspicion and constant competition are just some of the elements of diplomatic practice attributed to this period of Italian history.

The principle of placing state interests above ethical considerations emerged ever more strongly during this era and is forever associated with the work of the Venetian, Niccolò Machiavelli. In *The Prince*, Machiavelli states that what he describes is not a doctrine of government; rather it is the purpose of government at its most cynical and as he observed it in his own lifetime. Ironically, it seems that posterity took it as a doctrine for politics and diplomacy with quite dire consequences.

In the 1600s, Cardinal Richelieu of France made a major contribution to the development of diplomatic practice. Richelieu advocated that diplomacy should aim for long-term and durable relationships, not just opportunistic moments. Even failed negotiations, he said, are worthwhile experiences. Still placing the interests of the state above all other considerations, he taught the importance of strategic alliances, even with the most unpleasant partners, in the face of a common enemy.

Richelieu was also the first to make use of public opinion as a vehicle for political action. At a time when literacy was increasing, Richelieu was the first to use mass media – small printed pamphlets – for domestic propaganda. He further introduced a strong element of certainty in diplomatic negotiations, first, by insisting that negotiators must not exceed the instructions of the sovereign, and second, by stating that the utmost care must be taken when negotiating a treaty, for once signed and ratified, it had to be observed in its minutest detail. This element of certainty introduced two principles that are the cornerstones of diplomatic activity to this day: that by drawing up treaties through careful negotiations, no loopholes or misunderstandings are possible which might undermine the agreement at a later date; and that all parties to the negotiation are aware from the outset that their counterparts are the *authorised representatives* of their state, so all treaties are binding and effective *between states*. Thus in western history, by the seventeenth century, inter-state diplomatic relations had developed complex, formal structures.

Collective Security – General Assemblies and Princely Leagues

Concurrently, as the general practice of diplomacy and dealings with neighbouring and distant states increased through time, so did concepts and ideas relating to *collective security* issues in Europe. Throughout the Middle Ages, the Renaissance and until the late eighteenth century, much of Christian Europe's general sense of insecurity and fear arose from the presence of a strong Muslim Ottoman empire rampaging across its eastern borders. Suggestions of collective security, in the form of a league of European princes, each with a representative at a general assembly and a right to vote on assembly policies, date back to 1462.[7] Not altogether dissimilar to the NATO of five centuries later, the aim of this general assembly would have been to maintain peace between its members and protect each other against attack by non-members. Each member was to have its own army, paid for through domestic taxes. A wider network of officials, archives, seals, a single currency and even an international court were also envisaged. But despite the detailed outlining of the structures and function of such an assembly, no such scheme was ever formed. The Europe of 500 years ago was still too deeply divided.

In the seventeenth century two French essayists, the Duc de Sully and Emeric Crucé, produced yet further schemes for the advancement of world peace. To promote peace, Crucé[8] called for a congress of ambassadors representing not only the princes of Europe but also those of non-Christian states across the world – from the Ottomans to the Chinese, Tartars, Indians, Persians, Japanese, Ethiopians, Moroccans and others. The aim of the General Assembly would be for these princes to agree to communal protection and security. His belief was that through communication and mutual understanding, disputes and differences amongst states could be resolved without recourse to violence. Crucé attributed much importance to increased trade links and technological developments such as canal-building schemes as unifying and pacifying forces. But like so much else, his ideas were well before his time, and the scheme was left aside as Europe endured 300 more years of war.

Only in the nineteenth century following the French Revolution and the outbreak of the Napoleonic Wars did Europe's sense of international security change radically. It took well over a decade for Europe's powers to join forces against Napoleon's French empire, and finally defeat him at Waterloo in 1814. The quadripartite alliance of the kingdoms of Austria, Prussia, Britain and Russia held the Congress of Vienna to re-establish the territorial boundaries of pre-Napoleonic Europe. The Congress proved successful, not only in restoring the territorial boundaries of each state, but also in re-establishing the balance of power in Europe, which resulted in 40 years of inter-state peace.

The notion of a balance of power became prominent amongst the five European powers throughout the nineteenth century. The key to foreign policy for each state was to ensure that no single one, nor any alliance between them, could threaten the affairs of Europe as a whole. However, no sustained efforts were made to link Europe further together with the explicit aim of war prevention.

As the century progressed the interests and objectives of each state also changed. Russia took on an expansionist approach towards Turkey, and the unification of Germany and of Italy led to an imbalance in power relations. With the Germans suspicious of Russia, and the French suspicious of the Austrians and the Germans, mistrust was rife amongst these one-time allies. By 1914 the pragmatic and fluid alliances initiated in 1814 had become rather formal and rigid agreements. On both sides actions against either partnership meant the immediate military mobilisation of the other. Europe had effectively become a powder keg awaiting only a spark to ignite it. When it finally happened in Sarajevo with the assassi-nation of Archduke Ferdinand, heir to the Austro-Hungarian empire, the entire continent and the colonial offshoots were plunged into the First World War. Within four years eight million people had died and much of Europe lay in ruins.

The Birth of Modern 'Open' Diplomacy

Modern 'open' diplomacy as evidenced by the UN system first came into existence at the end of the First World War. Horrified and disillusioned by the secrecy and hidden motives which drove the world to war, President Woodrow Wilson presented a 14-point peace settlement. The main features included a call for the principle of self-determination, a reduction in armaments, the abolition of secret diplomacy and the formation of the League of Nations, where 'open covenants were openly arrived at'. Declaring that the rule of justice 'plays no favourites and knows no standards but the equal rights of the several people concerned',[9] he introduced the idea of egalitarianism amongst all sovereign nations to the international arena. It meant that the opinions and votes of every state were equally valid, irrespective of their size, military or economic power. The principle of non-interference in the domestic affairs of a sovereign state was also incorporated into the League's Charter.

Unfortunately, the League never succeeded. The defeated powers, Germany, Austria-Hungary, Turkey and Bulgaria, were not invited to the Versailles conference. Instead they were presented with the terms of the agreement as a *fait accompli* and effectively forced to sign the treaty. Germany withdrew resentfully, only to re-emerge even stronger 20 years later. Italy, who had fought on the allied side, felt cheated of territory that was promised to her in 1915. Russia, still immersed in a civil war, was not present, and the Bolshevik government was not recognised. The United States, which had initiated the whole process, withdrew from the negotiations as Congress refused to ratify the US's entry into the League. Wilson's defeat in the 1920 US presidential election was the final nail in the League's coffin.

The United Nations

Despite the failure of the League of Nations and the outbreak of the Second World War, the idea of 'open' diplomacy became an established part of diplomatic practice. Moreover, as the true horrors of the Second World War became apparent – the Nazis' genocide of the Jews and systematic killings of Poles, Russians and gypsies, and the terrifying destruction wrought by the atomic bombs dropped on Hiroshima and Nagasaki – the world was catapulted into a new era. The need for an international forum was recognised even more profoundly. So 300 years after Crucé first mooted his ideas, the notion of a world diplomatic arena, where a stronger and wider system of collective security was encouraged, became a reality. For the architects of the United Nations the existence of nuclear weapons added a further dimension of concern: the prevention of a future world war went hand-in-hand with the preservation of humanity as a whole.

In creating this new framework, the lofty ideals of the League were combined with hard realities, as Roosevelt demanded that executive power of the organisation be in the hands of the permanent members of the Security Council, comprising Great Britain, the United States, the Soviet Union, China[10] and France. Once again the principle of equilibrium was brought to bear, as the two new superpowers were balanced by two declining world powers and an increasingly important Asian nation. Founded on the principle of recognising the sovereign rights of the state, and on the assumption that the state represented its people, the organisation's mandate made explicit reference to 'eliminating the scourge of war'.

Preamble of the United Nations Charter[11]

WE THE PEOPLES
OF THE UNITED NATIONS,
DETERMINED

to save succeeding generations from the scourge of war, which twice in our lifetime has brought untold sorrow to mankind, and
to reaffirm faith in fundamental human rights, in the dignity and worth of the human person, in equal rights of men and women and of nations large and small, and

to establish conditions under which justice and respect for the obligations arising from treaties and other sources of international law can be maintained, and
to promote social progress and better standards of life in larger freedom,

AND FOR THESE ENDS

to practise tolerance and live together in peace with one another as good neighbours, and
to unite our strengths to maintain international peace and security, and
to ensure, by the acceptance of principles and the institution of methods, that armed force shall not be used, save in the common interest, and
to employ international machinery for the promotion of the economic and social advancement of all peoples,

HAVE RESOLVED TO
COMBINE OUR EFFORTS
TO ACCOMPLISH THESE AIMS.

The new institution was born in 1944 when representatives from 50 states accepted the key elements: a Security Council, a General Assembly, a permanent Secretariat, and a Secretary General. The executive was given authority to enforce its will, and all member states were obliged to accept the Council's decisions, including those requiring the use of armed forces. The granting of the power of veto to the permanent members was the only restrictive element in the Council's procedures, but it was one which was used only too often by the US and USSR over the next 50 years.

The presence of permanent delegates at the UN headquarters in New York has influenced traditional bilateral diplomacy and new 'open' diplomacy. On the one hand, by virtue of being in close proximity delegates have the opportunity of strengthening both formal and informal contacts. The existence of delegations at the UN has provided an essential and convenient means of attempting to resolve disputes and open channels of communication, especially amongst hostile states with no *official* diplomatic contact. Undoubtedly, even delegates of the most ostracised nations hold private talks with their American or European counterparts, despite the official and very public freeze on diplomatic ties. On the other hand, by virtue of the fact that the debating sessions themselves are widely televised and reported on, states have become more answerable to criticism from home. There is little doubt that the fist-banging or verbal bombardments that have characterised much of the Security Council's history have helped to reduce real tensions.

The recognition of all states on an equal basis also resulted in dramatic changes throughout the period of decolonisation in the 1960s. Suddenly a wealth of new states, some extremely poor and weak, found a voice on the world stage. The impact this had on both the US and the USSR was quite marked, as the new states could often sway votes and influence the general status quo. The sheer size and number of participatory states within the UN system have given it a strong degree of legitimacy, so much so that recognition from the UN is an important accolade for even the most despotic rulers.

The importance of economic and social development as a condition for sustainable peace was not lost on Roosevelt, Truman or Churchill. The Economic and Social Council (ECOSOC), the International Monetary Fund (IMF) and the International Bank for Reconstruction and Development (IBRD) were founded with the specific aims of achieving international financial stability, assisting in the reconstruction of war-ravaged economies and promoting world trade. Indeed, at the first signs of an expansionist Russian threat, the Americans conceived the Marshall Plan under which massive economic aid was offered to fund the reconstruction of any European nation destroyed during the war. Sixteen Western European nations accepted, forming the Organisation for European Economic Co-operation (OEEC) in 1948.[12]

The formation of other UN agencies, particularly in the fields of health, social welfare, culture and education, further expanded the boundaries of traditional diplomacy to incorporate a good deal more than just political manoeuvring. Also, it is important to recognise that the UN system, although based on state sovereignty, formally acknowledged the role that non-governmental organisations (NGOs) could play, particularly in the field of social justice and economic development.[13] Over the past 50 years, this has led to a phenomenal growth in the number and variety of NGOs throughout the world. The elaborate web of networks and agencies emerging in social, economic, scientific, cultural, humanitarian and medical fields has increased communication and co-operation not just between states, but also between peoples, to a level barely dreamt of before.

The UN's existence has influenced the erosion of absolute sovereignty over the years. In every field, from agreements on maritime activities and international air traffic controls to environmental issues and even international crime, numerous conventions have been passed and agreed on by the General Assembly. The emergence of regional and sub-regional organisations has led to even further devolutions of state power and a gradual erosion of absolute sovereignty. Member states have come under considerable pressure to comply with international conventions even when they conflict with their personal ambitions. Finally, in relation to the peaceful settlement of disputes, there is little doubt that the UN system and each Secretary General over the years have introduced and developed a series of diverse and highly effective 'tools' and 'approaches' to dispute resolution.

Tools for the Peaceful Settlement of Disputes[14]

1. *Negotiations and Consultations*: involve only the state parties to a dispute – who can initiate and monitor every phase as they deem appropriate. Negotiations can be applied to all kinds of disputes: legal, political or technical. Consultations are a variety of negotiations and involve initial discussions and 'exchange of views' between parties.

2. *Inquiry*: an inquiry is regarded as an impartial third party procedure for fact-finding and investigation. In an international dispute where there is disagreement on points of fact, states may initiate an 'inquiry' to establish the facts and other aspects of a dispute.

3. *Good Offices*: when states are unable to resolve a dispute mutually, a third party may offer his 'good offices' as a means of facilitating efforts, so that there is no further deterioration of the dispute. The third party may encourage the resumption of talks or provide alternative solutions.

4. *Mediation*: mediation occurs when a third party intervenes to reconcile claims of the disputants and offer a mutually acceptable proposal.

5. *Conciliation*: the task of a conciliation commission is to clarify the contentious issues, gather the necessary information and seek to bring the parties to an agreement. After the case is examined, the commission informs the parties of the terms of the agreement that it believes are suitable and gives a time frame for the parties to decide.

6. *Arbitration*: this is a process wherein states select judges to act on their behalf, with respect to the law. Disputants are legally bound to comply with the results of an arbitration procedure.

7. *Judicial Settlement*: state parties to a dispute may refer their dispute to a pre-constituted international court or tribunal composed of independent judges to settle their claims on the basis of international law. Disputants are legally bound to comply with any decisions reached.

8. *Resort to Regional Agencies or Arrangements*: if a dispute threatens regional security, regional inter-state agencies may become involved to regulate relations and establish regional arrangements.

9. *Secretary General's Good Office Function*: the UNSG can offer his/her good offices to seek a solution to a dispute by personal consultations, the despatch of a special representative and direct negotiations.

By offering member states the opportunity to select and implement procedures best suited to the settlement of their particular disputes, these developments have helped increase compliance with international laws and strengthen the culture of peaceful dispute resolution.

Constraints of the United Nations

Unfortunately the idealistic intentions which gave birth to the UN and which are laid out in its Charter have not always been rigorously enforced or respected. Human rights laws are flouted by many states, and the principle of self-interest is too often the driving force behind foreign policy decisions. Over the years Security Council members have periodically used their power and influence to further their own interests, at the cost of others. In particular during the Cold War years, the US and USSR in effect waged a 'third world war' through the many proxy civil wars and conflicts in the territories of other states.

Even in the case of inter-state wars, the UN has sometimes failed to intervene with sufficient determination and commitment. The Iran–Iraq war which lasted eight years and claimed over a million lives was a case in point. At the time even Iraq's patently illegal use of chemical weapons against innocent civilians prompted no decisive action from the General Assembly and the Security Council.

Self-Interest and State Interest
Failure to End the Iran–Iraq War

For the Iraqi state the opportunity to launch an attack to claim long-disputed territory from Iran, when the latter was experiencing internal political turmoil, was too great to forgo. Iran's retaliation and subsequent early success, however, were not sufficient for the leaders of the new Islamic regime. Under the banner of Islam and with a view to exporting their version of their revolution, they continued to fight. Both governments benefited from the war by focusing their nation's attention on the external enemy, while simultaneously strengthening their own dictatorial hold internally.

The war was also beneficial to western countries in pursuit of their own national interests. On the one hand, their interests were economic, as they were selling arms to both states and making large profits. On the other hand, they had political interests as well, for both Iran and Iraq were regarded as dangerous nations, with excessive military power. By staying at war for so long, they were effectively neutralising each other's military capabilities and limiting each other's political and economic influence in a highly volatile region. So trench warfare and regular urban bombings continued for eight years, leaving the civilians and soldiers of both nations to suffer the consequences.

Moreover, the issues to arise in the post-Cold War world reveal further problems within the UN system, namely the difficulties in tackling internal conflicts and civil wars effectively. Since traditional diplomatic practices have been predominantly concerned with the relationship of separate states, the prevention, management and resolution of *internal* conflicts or 'domestic affairs' of one state were rarely the concern or responsibility of another. Given that the UN system is predicated on the principle of non-interference in a state's 'domestic affairs', it has no mandate to intervene in internal conflicts without the express invitation and consent of the state or unless the UNSC deems there is a danger to international peace and security.[15]

This inevitably creates problems. For although in the past UN representatives have successfully intervened in the internal conflicts of countries such as El Salvador and Guatemala, more often than not the UN is trapped in a paradox. On the one hand, the organisation is entrusted with the responsibility of ensuring international peace and security. On the other hand, its own mandate proscribes it from intervention in the internal affairs of a member state without prior consent and invitation. The question therefore is, can the UN override the wishes of the governments of its member states to intervene and mediate in a conflict where the disenfranchised population are challenging the legitimacy of that government? Given that the structures of diplomatic negotiations and the UN's tools for mediation are primarily applicable when the disputants have mutual veto power or equal legitimacy, does the organisation have the means to intervene adequately? For as discussed in Chapter 2, in the context of internal conflicts the relationship is often asymmetrical, which means that disputants do not have equal political legitimacy, nationally or internationally. Without a level playing field, the chances of a successful resolution to the conflict are severely reduced.

Yet the attempt to create a 'level playing field' gives rise to numerous other dilemmas. If efforts are made to contact the insurgency movement, it may appear that the UN is legitimising a group which could have minority support in the country. These actions not only undermine the government's trust in the UN, but could exacerbate the conflict. In other words, as mentioned in Chapter 3, intervention could have a perverse effect on the conflict situation. But the opposite also holds true. If the UN does acknowledge the insurgents' role, then they may be unwilling to accept the UN as a mediator. In part these dilemmas can be addressed by exploring more appropriate and acceptable means of gaining consent and access to all parties. In other words, what is the optimal time for intervention, before violence breaks out or later on? When does it become absolutely necessary? Who should intervene at which stage? These issues are currently being explored by the UN and other international institutions.

Pitched into a New Era – The UN's Recent Developments

As discussed in Chapter 1, Boutros Boutros-Ghali explicitly stated in his *Agenda for Peace* that the organisation needed to take *a more preventive and proactive role* in the preservation of peace, the peaceful settlements of disputes and the restoration of confidence in the aftermath of *internal* conflict.

Preventive diplomacy he said, involved 'action to prevent disputes from arising between parties, to prevent existing disputes from escalating into conflicts and to limit the spread of the latter when they occur'.[16] Involvement by *one state* in the affairs of another is nothing new in international affairs. But in the context of *intergovernmental organisations*, which are founded on the principle of state sovereignty, unwarranted intervention, particularly in domestic politics, is still taboo. So although his ideas did not emerge in a vacuum (as in part he was calling for the implementation of existing provisions for the protection of human rights), Boutros-Ghali was also venturing into uncharted territory.

In practice, however, not enough was done to explore non-military options or to adapt existing mediation mechanisms to situations of internal conflict. Preventive action became synonymous with military action and peace enforcement. No distinctions were made between the prevention, management or resolution of a conflict. International peacekeeping troops with unclear mandates were sent to crisis points. Although there were notable successes as in Macedonia, it was the failures that grabbed the headlines. Somalia, Bosnia and Rwanda undermined Boutros-Ghali's proactivism, leading to a crisis of confidence within the organisation as a whole. By 1996 few states were willing to offer their troops for missions in Burundi or Zaire.

What Alternatives Exist? Non-state Actors

So, we arrive at the heart of this discussion and our current position in the continuum of diplomatic and international relations. Given the limitations of existing international structures, how can they be improved and developed to take account of recent changes? What other action should be taken, and by whom, to tackle violent and deadly internal conflicts? How can such conflicts be prevented? What mechanisms are needed to manage a conflict, to ensure it does not escalate further? What approaches could be explored to attempt their resolution?

In our previous discussions we made reference to the increase in 'multipolarity' and complexity of the international arena in recent years. In other words, beyond the framework of state-based actors, there is a wealth of non-state groups emerging as protagonists on the world's political and economic stage. Some, of course, are perpetrators of armed conflict challenging existing status quos. But a multitude of others – religious groups, NGOs, community groups, other forms of citizen-based entities and even transnational corporations – have emerged as significant players in the socio-economic realms of the international arena.

Growth of the Non-State Sector[17]

Modernity: communications and information technology, vast movements of people across borders, inexpensive air travel, growing diaspora communities, increasing global economic interdependency, all contributing to the growth of an international civil society. State boundaries are becoming ever-more porous, and absolute state power and control of society are diminishing, even under the most oppressive systems of government. Unable or unwilling to bear the burden of social welfare and development single-handedly, states are curtailing their activities, to support and encourage more efficient private initiatives to take over the responsibilities.

In 1996 an estimated 3,000 development non-governmental organisations (NGOs) from OECD countries controlled and dispersed up to US$ 5.7 billion per year in assistance to developing countries. They work in partnership with an estimated 10,000–20,000 'southern' NGOs, which in turn assist up to 100 million people a year. Parallel to these organisations, there has been a veritable explosion in the growth of grassroots organisations (GROs), which focus particularly on the provision of health, education, credit services and so forth.[18]

Given the wider context of the post-Cold War era and the dominance of neo-liberal economics and liberal democratic theory in social and economic policy forums, this rise of NGOs and GROs is not accidental. For donor governments, their support of such independent organisations falls in line with the belief that private initiatives are more efficient than government-controlled programmes. It is believed that private initiatives, either as grassroots work or as NGOs have always been better at reaching the poorest sectors of society. Furthermore, from the perspective of democratic industrialised nations of the West/North, NGOs and GROs are efficient vehicles for the creation of a healthy and active civil society which can counterbalance state powers and encourage democratic ideals and the participation of citizens in public life.

The rise of citizen-based movements and the burgeoning of international networks of citizen-based groups are not solely the results of development aid policies. They have grown out of a complex combination of events, from the expansion of information and communications technology, which allows disparate groups across the world to communicate with each other, to disillusionment with political ideologies and a fervent belief that individuals can make a difference in the world.

Perhaps it is fair to say that finally 'the people' of the United Nations are indeed taking action and calling for greater account-ability from their states in the wider global arena. Instead of rejecting the system, non-state actors such as minority groups are optimising their access to official channels and straining to get their voices heard on the global stage. The rationale for people's par-ticipation in local and global political affairs is grounded in the experiences of daily life. Those surrounded by poverty and squalor, or witnessing environmental degradation at the hands of their governments or international companies, are the first to strive for improvement and a better life, just as those who live amidst the dire realities of conflict and violence are the first to crave peace.

In recent years a number of international and local NGOs have been formed with the explicit aim of tackling issues related to intra-state conflicts and filling the void which their more official counterparts have left. The involvement of NGOs and grassroots organisations in conflict resolution or peacemaking efforts is, however, still very new. Indeed there are still very few organisa-tions *dedicated* to mediation work. Yet these organisations have certain advantages which, when used in conjunction with the UN and other intergovernmental organisations (IGOs), can be critical in facilitating negotiations processes. Most importantly, such NGOs do not have wider political affiliations to any states or parties. Those that are professional are careful to protect their impartiality. They do not seek overt recognition for their work. Rather, they take advantage of their relative anonymity to work more discreetly. As a result they are not under pressure to secure a 'quick-fix' solution to the conflict. Often such organisations, at both the local and inter-national level, have a long-term commitment to peacemaking efforts. They do not have the eyes of the world on them and consequently can be more flexible in their approach. They are better able to gain access to rebel or insurgency movements by virtue of working or living amongst them and, once in contact, can build relationships based on mutual trust and understanding.

At the height of a conflict, essentially in the *pre-negotiations* phase when there is no communication between opposing sides, NGOs can be instrumental in creating spaces for informal dialogue. They can encourage moderate voices to come together to find issues of mutual concern and agreement. They can bring the experiences of other conflict situations to the table, thus exposing parties to different solutions. They can help identify the most intractable and complex issues, thereby contributing to the wider policies for mediation. NGOs can also facilitate the pre-negotiations process by providing technical assistance and helping to create the framework and agenda for the official talks to take place.

Where official talks break down, NGOs can continue their behind-the-scenes work to generate new initiatives. They can provide training to develop the capacities of local communities and local leaders for negotiations. By working with key individuals from either side, NGOs can generate greater awareness and understanding of each group's positions and claims to the other. Moreover, by having access to a wider international arena, NGOs can be instrumental in alerting and informing the world of 'forgotten conflicts', in helping to catalyse the necessary assistance and action, and in providing advice on policy formulation with regard to particular regions. Finally, in places such as Northern Ireland, NGOs have played a determining factor in the strengthening of civil society and the involvement of wide cross-sections of the population in concrete peace-building programmes. In effect they have generated 'peace coalitions' across different sectors of society.

Table 4.1 State v. Non-state Diplomacy

State-based diplomacy based on:	Non-state diplomacy based on:
Perceived self-interests	People-to-people relations
State-to-state relations	Trust building, networking and solidarity
Sovereignty and non-interference in internal affairs	Long-term commitment
Reliance on UN, and IGOs and bilateral governmental diplomatic relations	Low-profile foundation building
Short-termist approach	Flexibility and creativity

Basic Observations on Third Party Intervention

It is rare for any third party mediation to take place before the violence has spiralled out of control. (An interesting adjunct to this point is that given that parties tend to be more amenable to dialogue before the outbreak of violence, there is no doubt that numerous potential wars have been resolved peacefully. Yet because they did not happen, we never hear of them. In other words, the prevention of war is a great non-event.)

Intervention depends largely on two important factors: whether the UN has a mandate to involve itself, and whether there is sufficient political will from within the international community. The principle of sovereignty and non-interference in a nation's domestic affairs can effectively restrict the UN's role to that of a concerned observer. The situation in Algeria is a prime example (despite the estimated scores of deaths each week, the rejection of its offers of mediation has left the international community powerless to help prevent the killings).

The question of political will is less clear-cut and more unpredictable. When security and economic interests are threatened, the international community can be swiftly galvanised into action. Where there is no such threat, intervention frequently relies on pressure exerted by the wider public or pressure groups and lobbies. Unfortunately, the consequences of intervening in such an arbitrary and spontaneous fashion can be disastrous. America's determination to enter Somalia, for example, had more to do with intense lobbying from pressure groups in Washington, a constant stream of images of hunger on CNN and concern for public opinion at home, than what was ultimately the best solution for Somalia. Did the humanitarian objective of Operation Restore Hope succeed? The response is different from every quarter. Some accuse the US of tipping the local balance of power with their intervention. Others suggest that confusion regarding the forces' mandate led to the débâcle. The mission ended when the death of American soldiers sparked enough outrage at home to pressure the US administration to pull out. So even with political will, ad hoc interventions lacking clear objectives or understanding of a situation can exacerbate a crisis.

Rarely these days can a single government or international organisation act independently in any field without repercussions elsewhere. For despite their self-interested pursuits, the existence of multinational organisations such as the UN and EU, not to mention the numerous other economic alliances, has made most governments dependent on others in the international community. When it comes to tackling complex internal conflicts this interdependence is further magnified.

Consequently we argue that there should be a more *structured* approach to prevention rather than the chaotic arrangements which exist at the moment. There should be a more ordered means of identifying the causes of conflict and devising multilateral policies and solutions. In this way the sense of inevitability associated with many long term internal conflicts would be reduced.

In the medical world, epidemiologists conduct detailed analyses of the changes in the development of diseases. Systems exist which allow for early predictions of an epidemic, and response mechanisms are put in place to contain the outbreak or to immunise the vulnerable sectors of society. Doctors can predict the likelihood of a measles epidemic amongst children on a cyclical basis, advertising campaigns are mounted to give early warning and vaccinations are provided.

A culture of *preventive action* has permeated through society. It is the norm to take health care seriously and, when necessary, to take preventive medication (e.g. vaccinations).[19] Furthermore, chemists, biologists, nurses, doctors, specialists, hospitals, emergency, intensive care, post-operative and rehabilitation units are part of the system. Even the state and the commercial sector which provide different levels of insurance to cover illness expenses are involved. Moreover, medical care encompasses a referral system whereby a general practitioner diagnoses and refers a patient to more specialist care when necessary. So the risks and burden of illness are shared across many sectors of society and at every stage of the crisis.

The structures necessary for conflict prevention also require the involvement of a range of activities, specialists and treatments. In other words, it is important for governments and IGOs to work in conjunction with NGOs and other non-state groups. Each sector should recognise the expertise and comparative advantages of the others at every stage of a conflict. In this way all efforts are optimised, and there is coherence and a shared understanding of the situation.

Burden-Sharing

The greater the level of co-operation and co-ordination, the greater the degree of accountability and sustainability of the actions that are taken. In other words, if the UN, the EU, individual governments, the media and a host of NGOs focus on a particular conflict, undertaking different tasks aimed at resolving or alleviating the violence, there is mutual pressure to be accountable to each other and to sustain their efforts despite difficulties.

The aim here is to share the burden of conflict by utilising the expertise of the mediators to address the critical issues and concerns of the belligerents involved in the conflict. By creating an international umbrella of concern focused on the resolution of the conflict, disputing parties would have a chance to voice their opinions, while mediators and facilitators address the component factors which together make the conflict intractable. It is also a means of ensuring that each party is accountable to a wider international community, and so must keep their side of the bargain. The more the burden is shared, the less the likelihood of one party pulling out, and the greater the chance of the conflict being contained or expressed in less violent terms. In other words, sharing the burden can help transform the conflict situation.

In Bosnia, for example, NATO is providing just such a protective umbrella. Under the auspices of the NATO Stabilisation Force (S-For) other groups, including UN agencies, humanitarian and development NGOs, grassroots community groups, the OSCE, the EU and others, are striving to consolidate and implement the Dayton Peace Accord. In the Middle East too such an umbrella of concern exists. The United States has played a major role in attempting to create a framework for the resolution of the conflict, and maintaining international focus on the region. Other efforts such as the work of the Norwegian academics and the government which led to the Oslo Accord, as well as internal Palestinian and Israeli initiatives, have been critical in driving the process forward. The EU and a number of Arab states have provided financial aid and advice, while neighbouring Arab states, such as Egypt and Jordan, have played an important role in balancing and tempering the discussions at each stage. It is the combination of forces that gives the agreements legitimacy, pushes the parties towards the negotiations table even during the worst times, and makes them accountable to a wider international community.

Figure 4.1 Umbrella of Concern

This is not to say that peace comes easily, or indeed that any agreement reached will be upheld by all parties at all times. Nor can we ignore the opposition forces that may exist to any peace negotiations, as Hamas and extremist Jewish groups have demonstrated.[20] The simple point is that the chances of successfully resolving a dispute are much higher if national and international agencies and organisations can be persuaded to combine their efforts with each one adopting different but complementary approaches. The Middle East may still be in turmoil, but efforts are still being made to sustain the peace-building process. No such efforts or concerns even exist yet in the case of Afghanistan or Sri Lanka.

Multi-track Diplomacy

Central to this discussion is the concept of *multi-track diplomacy* and *positive peace*. Defined as the application of peacemaking from different vantage points within a network,[21] multi-track diplomacy is based on two principles. The first is that the greater the degree of concern and effort there is to prevent or resolve a conflict, the greater the chance of success. The second is that the limitations of each actor or sector can be overcome through co-operation and co-ordination with others. The concept of multi-track diplomacy evolved from a growing realisation that the mechanisms and structures of peacemaking developed by the international community during the Cold War years were no longer adequate to deal with the changing nature of post-Cold War conflicts. This point was tacitly conceded in 1995 with the publication of Boutros Boutros-Ghali's *Supplement to an Agenda for Peace* which admitted the UN's limitations in meeting the demands for the use of force in internal conflict, not least because of the severe financial constraints imposed on the organisation. Yet beyond the practical obstacles, there also lie a number of more conceptual issues related to the nature and complexity of internal conflicts, which multi-track diplomacy attempts to address.

As discussed above, official state-based diplomatic manoeuvres are often circumscribed by political interests, a lack of trust, short-term domestic considerations and an inability or unwillingness to address the depth and complexity of social and economic problems caused by internal conflict. To address some of these shortcomings, some official diplomatic missions are already complemented by unofficial second-track efforts involving more low-profile and longer-term activities. Unofficial efforts have the advantage of giving disputants the opportunity of communication, and 'talks before talks' without the risk of a public loss of face. The multi-track approach widens the diplomatic process even further, to incorporate

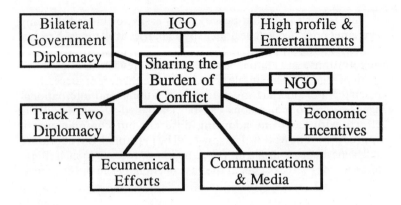

Figure 4.2 Multi-track Diplomacy

the work of non-state and local actors as well. Non-governmental or citizen-based activities can be very effective in the arduous process of trust-building and creating a space for dialogue, but may not have the necessary resources or political leverage to bring about real change single-handedly. Yet the combined force of these approaches can address the fundamental issues and still bring the necessary political momentum. In other words, every initiative has a limited but critical impact, and to be effective it must be combined with other efforts.

Intergovernmental diplomacy

Organisations such as the UN, EU, Organisation of African Unity (OAU), Association of South East Asian Nations (ASEAN), OSCE or the North Atlantic Treaty Organisation (NATO) can set a framework under which diplomatic activities are conducted. The Office of High Commissioner on National Minorities within the OSCE is a noted example of successful, quiet, high-level diplomacy in Latvia, Khazakistan, and Kyrgyzstan, Ukraine and Macedonia amongst other places. The High Commissioner's mandate is to intervene before the outbreak of violence and conflict and to provide technical assistance in conflict resolution and institution-building.

These umbrella organisations can also act as a deterrent to the escalation of violent conflict, by agreeing to intervene if and when the potential for violence increases. However, member states must also ensure that internationally recognised human rights treaties and humanitarian law are adhered to by all. Using existing political or economic relations, a potential or on-going conflict can be introduced into official discussions, and a more proactive stance can be taken to resolve the dispute.

Governmental Peacemaking

Bilateral negotiations can draw upon historical or existing relations, and individual countries can act as mediators between warring factions. As we have seen, superpower involvement in the Middle East was complemented by the mediating role of a smaller Norwegian government which was trusted for its neutrality.

Small to medium-powered nations such as the Scandinavian countries and Canada can play an important role in encouraging dialogue or mediating in internal conflicts. These states are not tainted by a history of colonial exploits, and are therefore regarded as impartial actors. Their incentive for involvement in conflicts is not based on strategic interests, but on their desire to maintain their standing within the international community.

Regional states also have an important function, as they often have a better understanding of the conflict situation, and perhaps a greater commitment to the peace process as their own stability can be affected when war exists in their region. For example, Côte d'Ivoire was involved in mediation between warring factions in Sierra Leone, and Tanzania is bringing disputants in the Burundi conflict together.

Second-track Efforts

'Track two' or 'second-track' diplomacy is defined as 'unofficial, informal interaction between members of adversarial groups or nations which aims to develop strategies, influence public opinion and organise human and material resources in ways that resolve their conflict'.[22] It is not a substitute for official 'track one' bilateral government or leader-to-leader channels. It aims to complement track one diplomacy with its emphasis on relationships and policy changes generated through lower political levels. The involvement of former President Carter in Haiti or North Korea in 1994, or the initial secret negotiations undertaken by the Norwegian FAFO with tacit support from their government in the Middle East, are examples of semi-official second-track diplomacy. Away from the media spotlight, second-track diplomacy avoids embarrassment or 'losing face' for all sides and can be useful in setting an agenda for official talks.

In 1995 while the conflict between the military government and the Revolutionary United Front (RUF/SL) raged in Sierra Leone, the IGOs involved, the OAU, UN and Commonwealth Secretariat, had no means of contacting the rebel group. Since the RUF/SL were holding a number of foreign and national hostages, the international community was unwilling to initiate any form of dialogue. International Alert (IA), a UK-based NGO, was able to establish radio contact with the rebels, and arrange for face-to-face meetings. Following a 300-mile trek through the bush and a series of discussions, the hostages were released into IA's care and taken to the Guinean border, where they were met by the International Committee for the Red Cross ICRC. These events provided a significant opportunity for communication between the warring groups and helped bring the RUF/SL to the negotiating table.

In South Africa during the critical period leading up to the 1994 elections, disagreements between Inkatha, the ANC and the government threatened the entire transition process. Official international envoys, Lord Carrington and Henry Kissinger were unable to resolve the dispute and left the country in dismay. But at the eleventh hour, Professor Washington Okumo, a Kenyan diplomat with stronger personal ties to the groups involved, was able to bring the disputants together. The success of his last-minute efforts led to a peaceful elections process.[23]

The objective of such efforts is to help build trust between the factions and the mediator, and develop lines of communication between the factions themselves. Given the intense polarisation and alienation which occurs through years of conflict, these second-track efforts are critical, as they allow for the development of a degree of consensus between disputants before public and political pressure to secure a treaty mounts.

Second-track Diplomacy – Former US President Carter in North Korea[24]

In mid-June 1994, the United States came much closer to waging war on the Korean peninsula than anyone except a handful of insiders understood at the time. The crisis arose when North Korea – after threatening for more than a year to withdraw from the Non-Proliferation Treaty, under which it pledged not to manufacture nuclear weapons – unloaded the nuclear material from its working reactor. The International Atomic Energy Agency, the UN office that monitors compliance with the treaty, objected strongly to North Korea's actions and sent a strongly worded report to the UN Security Council. This touched off a long-anticipated drive for UN sanctions against the reclusive communist state. In a formal statement, North Korea responded that 'sanctions mean war'.

In the midst of the discussion, President Clinton and his aides were interrupted by a telephone call from former President Jimmy Carter, who was in the North Korean capital Pyongyang on a self-initiated mission to resolve the nuclear impasse. Carter had gone to North Korea dismayed that no senior American had been to see President Kim Il Sung. After a lengthy discussion, Carter reported that the North Korean leader had agreed to freeze his nuclear programme and not to expel the IAEA. In return, Carter recommended that the drive for UN sanctions be dropped.

Carter's mission was the turning point. Thanks to the former president, 16 June 1994, can be remembered as the day a growing risk of war on the Korean peninsula was averted.

Ecumenical Efforts

Throughout history, religion has often been a cause of war and of repression. Even in the contemporary world religious dogma is used to instigate violence, and the church has often become embroiled in a conflict.[25] Yet religion and religious organisations can and do play a very significant role in initiating dialogue and building peace processes. The spiritual element that religious figures bring to negotiations can promote an environment conducive to dialogue and reconciliation. Religious figures are also often trusted by all sides and their suggestions respected. Furthermore, the existence of a global network and a hierarchical structure which reach all levels of society enables the work of local church and religious leaders to complement the peace process both at grassroots level and on a national or international scale.

Religious establishments such as the Society of Friends (the Quakers) or the Catholic Church can bring pressure and influence to bear on a wider spectrum. In Mozambique, for example, the Italian-based Catholic lay community of Sant' Egidio initiated the talks in 1990 which led to a ceasefire in 1992.[26] Sant' Egidio's members had personal contact and friendships with religious leaders in Mozambique. They had direct access to and the support of the Vatican and the Italian government. Prior to the talks process, they had established links and built trust with leaders of the rebel group Renamo. Before the talks became official, Sant' Egidio had offered its compound in Rome as a confidential venue for informal discussions. Finally, their impartiality and neutrality as mediators were never disputed.

During the Biafran War of 1967–70 in Nigeria, a Quaker mission led by Adam Curle played a pivotal role in the resolution of the conflict.[27] Maintaining a low-profile presence and in constant communication with both the Nigerian government and the Biafran representatives, they convinced the leaders to attend a peace conference even while the conflict raged. Although the Biafrans were a majority Muslim population, they trusted and believed in the Quakers' genuine desire for peace.

Similarly, during the 1980s, the Conciliation Commission in Nicaragua brought Indians and Sandinista fighters together under the banner of the Morovian Church, was an essential ingredient in the peace-building process. Throughout the conflict, the Commission remained committed to a peaceful settlement, and in turn acted as mediator, messenger, fund-raiser and spiritual guide.[28]

In South Africa much of the credit for the peaceful transition from apartheid to democratic rule is given to church movements who preached a message of tolerance, forgiveness and reconciliation. As an intrinsic part of the community, the church was in a unique position to mobilise support for a peace process. Its own record of humanitarian actions, set of moral and ethical values and commitment to society throughout the conflict and in the wake of a settlement revealed the immense potential that the ecumenical community could build upon.

Citizen and Community-based Efforts

Encouraging and supporting peace-building at all levels of a country which suffers from war is one of the strongest features of the multi-track approach. Citizen- and community-based efforts refers to the involvement of local people from different sectors of society in the peace process. It usually indicates grassroots involvement, but can also encompass 'mid-level' political initiatives. Although wars are often fought in the name of particular groups, and the civilian population is the most affected by the violence, their participation in resolving conflicts and restoring peace has often been limited or ignored. Yet citizen peacemakers can be an immensely powerful constituency.

There are numerous examples of citizen-based diplomacy. In Somalia, for example, clan elders have used traditional kinship networks to resolve conflicts. In Israel the 'Peace Now' group has been an effective voice of the Israeli and Palestinian people. During the 1980s in the Philippines, rural villages, schools and universities took a stand against the army and rebel forces by declaring peace zones and peace corridors. By the early 1990s, people's organisations, particularly those representing different social sectors – the peasants, urban workers, fisherfolk and a range of non-governmental organisations – joined to formulate an acceptable peace agenda outside the realms of official state politics.[29]

For years now in Northern Ireland, a wide range of community-based activities have been initiated to bridge sectarian divisions and enable citizens to voice their concerns and opinions about peace. By forming women's and children's groups and promoting community-based activities, they provide an opportunity for people to build personal relationships, dismantle defensive barriers and dispel negative images of one other. It is a process of building consensus, the will for peace and the momentum to progress amongst those most affected by the conflict.

Economic Incentives

Economic incentives can be offered through a number of channels. At a global level, the World Bank and IMF could (and are beginning to) take a more active stance in advocating conflict resolution and prevention as part of the conditions for the provision of aid. Development policy programmes are increasingly supporting peace-building and conflict resolution activities. Prominence is already being given to environmental programmes tackling problems such as water and land scarcity, desertification, pollution and other fundamental causes of conflict, but these projects need to be further expanded and developed.

Within intergovernmental organisations such as the EU whose policy is to help the *fostering of peace and stability, development, democracy and respect for human rights*,[30] the most effective use of resources is still being debated. The EU does fund a number of programmes, including elections monitoring and training in good governance throughout Eastern and Central Europe. But more resources could be allocated to programmes protecting minority groups, the poor and the marginalised. They should encourage the development of a democratic process and a greater commitment to a restriction on arms exports. They could also support peace education programmes and fund research into conflict issues.

International corporations and large multinational companies could also provide economic assistance. Many companies have a policy of providing charitable aid to the regions in which they invest, but invariably their commercial gains far outweigh any contributions they make. The corporate sector could be encouraged to fund programmes which focus on sustainable development or aim to mitigate conflicts. In areas of ethnic discrimination, they could operate a programme of 'positive discrimination' so that the more marginalised communities have access to jobs and training. They could contribute resources and materials such as office equipment, computers, technical expertise and training to sections of civil society. As they are potential or existing investors in a country, corporations could exert pressure on governments to work towards a peaceful resolution of a conflict. Additionally, companies could be encouraged to support publicly the principles of conflict prevention amongst others in the corporate sector and their own governments.

Of course, scepticism in business dictates that such actions would be unlikely, that corporations are unwilling participants in politics, especially publicly. Yet, by virtue of the difficulties and criticisms that British Petroleum (BP) and Shell have faced in relation to their work in Colombia and Nigeria, these two companies have already implemented certain measures. BP has engaged in multi-party talks with the Colombian government, community groups and NGOs in an effort to reduce levels of violence and reach a compromise with its counterparts, while Shell has promised to take more account of the views and suggestions of human rights and environmental groups when making policy decisions. The awareness that not only are peace and stability in their long-term interest, but that they as major economic actors have some leverage and can play a major role, is slowly being realised.

Media and Communications Participation

As mentioned in Chapter 3, the national and international media could be an effective vehicle in their analyses of political changes and provision of early warning information. The international media is a particularly powerful tool in mobilising public opinion and moulding the perceptions of policy-makers. It can have an enormous positive or negative impact on a conflict. Intensive coverage of the Bosnian conflict alerted the world to the daily atrocities that were occurring there. Public opinion gradually demanded intervention from the international political and military arena.

At the local level, however, the media is often exploited as an effective tool for propaganda by conflicting parties. In Rwanda *Le Radio des Milles Collines* was used to instigate and encourage the massacres. War reporting should aim to counter extremism and provide objective accounts. Local media in particular could be encouraged to call for calm and provide coverage of more moderate voices. Unbiased reporting is neither easy nor always possible, but local journalists could be trained to follow a code of conduct or journalistic ethos which encourages objectivity. Entertainment programmes such as soap operas and discussions could be used to promote ideas of tolerance and reconciliation through more personal channels. The US-based NGO Search for Common Ground, for example, has attempted to develop a soap opera for Burundian radio, in which the conflict is addressed within the context of the daily lives of ordinary people. Across Eastern Europe, another US-based organisation, the Open Society Fund, has provided financial assistance to independent radio stations which broadcast uncensored news.

Such initiatives could make a positive contribution in helping to create a space for dialogue and moderation. Mass media could also be used effectively to promote reconciliation and cross-community relations. National radio stations could broadcast open debates and public discussions on issues relating to the conflict. They could be used as a vehicle to promote understanding and share experiences between opposing groups.

Celebrities and Entertainments

By employing high-profile personalities with access to the media, it is possible to highlight the plight of war victims and raise funds for projects. The most obvious recent example of this was the phenomenal impact that Diana, Princess of Wales, had on the landmine campaign. Her association with the victims of landmines in countries such as Angola and Bosnia and her repeated calls for action on a global level succeeded in transforming an important but relatively unknown campaign into the most powerful and emotive issue of the day. The landmines treaty recently signed by 120 countries and the award of the 1997 Nobel Peace Prize to the International Campaign to Ban Landmines (ICBL) are in part a tribute to the work she did in highlighting the terrible suffering and destruction caused by landmines. Mother Teresa was another whose lifelong crusade to help the poor and the disenfranchised did so much to publicise the unimaginable squalor and misery endured by millions of people around the world. Other high-profile philanthropists include the financier George Soros who donates large sums of money to promote education and 'open societies' in many ex-communist states, and Ted Turner of CNN, who has pledged up to $1 billion to UN agencies. Celebrities unite to raise funds with the aim of providing sustainable development aid for the British-based Comic Relief charity. Entertainers could also be effective lobbyists calling for attention to 'forgotten wars' or joining together in advocating human rights issues. They could assist by influencing cultural policy towards the incorporation of peace education through the arts, linking with artists from areas of conflict, and visiting regions of potential conflict to bring greater awareness of the problems. They could also lend their names to peace initiatives, thereby making peacemaking more fashionable and accessible to the general public. International arts, music and film festivals could be organised with the aim of bringing greater exposure to the artists of different nations which suffer from conflict or with the view to exposing a wider audience to the issues relating to conflict.

Rather than offering compromise, appeasement or suppression, multi-track diplomacy aims to address and resolve the complexities of conflict by applying the appropriate action and involving different groups at each level of society. Ultimately, the objective is to ensure that every aspect of a conflict is dealt with, and that there is broad societal participation and burden-sharing in the dialogue and peace-building process (Figure 4.3).[31]

In relation to the Northern Ireland conflict, for example, at the top echelons or top end of the triangle in Figure 4.3, political parties and military leaders are involved in wide-ranging and general discussions. Process, timing and implementation of key agreements are decided. Relevant legislation or constitutional changes are agreed, and public statements and declarations are made. Without the participation of key individuals who represent a wider political party, the talks would not be possible. Furthermore, at this level a change in personalities can make a tremendous positive or negative impact. For example, in Britain the new Labour government led by Tony Blair, and the appointment of 'Mo' Mowlam as Secretary of State for Northern Ireland, has had a positive impact and resulted in a second ceasefire agreement. By contrast, in Israel Prime Minister Benjamin Netanyahu is himself seen by many to be detrimental to the talks process.[32]

Meanwhile amongst the middle ranks of society, the focus is on consensus-building and the expansion of spaces for dialogue between groups on either side of the divide. Be they eminent journalists, academics or religious leaders, their role is to ensure the terms of the peace talks are on the one hand, understood and accepted by the citizens, while on the other hand, that the citizens' voice is heard at the higher levels. Joint peace commissions can be

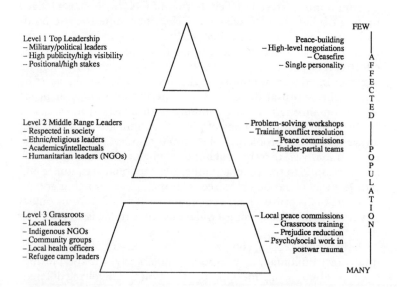

Figure 4.3 Creating Coalitions and Sharing the Burden

formed and training provided in problem-solving and conflict resolution. In Northern Ireland, the Women's Support Network has set an example of a citizen-based movement which has grown to national importance. From organising cross-community music festivals to running seminars and workshops on the role of women in peace-building, the network has created a public space in which women are given the opportunity to voice their opinions, take action and participate in the peace-building process.

Also at this level, humanitarian and human rights NGOs are active in monitoring ceasefire agreements, elections and ensuring that promises are kept. Respected members of the community can be involved in mediations and negotiations. Much of their work is in the form of discreet, low-profile and often informal dialogues, either with each party separately or on occasions jointly.

These groups also reach out to encourage grassroots movements and activities. From local health officials to community and welfare groups, the aim is to ensure that at the very heart of society, amongst those who suffer most in the conflict, there is consensus and support for the agreements being reached. At an individual and community level, it is necessary to work at reducing prejudices and fears of the 'other'.

Local community groups work to give a voice to the marginalised communities, so that their interests are not deliberately ignored for political purposes. Moreover, it is at this level that attention can be given to individuals suffering the traumas and losses of violent conflict. Orphans, widows, combatants, displaced peoples and returning refugees need to be resettled and given time to reintegrate into the community. In countries such as Mozambique and Angola where landmines still cover fields and transport routes, local community groups, with assistance and support from national and international groups, work to clear each area of mines.

In Northern Ireland, local community groups host public discussions on aspects of sectarian division on one hand, and sponsor sports events on the other. They provide opportunities for cross-community exchanges and educational programmes. They organise a range of joint projects from tackling issues such as HIV and AIDS, to organising public debates on the question of justice and policing.[33] Taken individually, such projects may seem of little consequence, but viewed within the wider context of the Northern Ireland conflict and peace process, their impact becomes clear. Each in their own way provides an opportunity for communities and individuals to communicate with and understand their counterparts. Through tackling issues of common concern or giving people the opportunity to share common interests, they help them to break through their fears and insecurities. By bringing the critical elements of the negotiations process such as the question of justice, the impact of the ceasefire or the Framework Document into a debate in the wider public domain, they give the communities most affected by the conflict an opportunity to participate in the peace process itself.

Third Party NGO Intervention – The Decision to Engage

The decision to engage in a conflict must be based on sound criteria and analysis. The background and historical context of the conflict must be established. Underlying factors such as the geographical or environmental context, social conditions and gender issues must be analysed. Local regional and international stakeholders must be identified. Based on these factors, the specific opportunities for transforming the conflict must be explored. Other activists in the field, be they local groups or international organisations must also be identified. Any new programmes should be devised to complement and add value to existing strategies.

Another critical question to be faced is whether a particular project or region falls within the competencies of an NGO. The point of entry into a conflict, consent from disputants and access to them are crucial. Identifying that point of entry and network of communications is fundamental. The strategy for involvement must also assess the comparative advantages that an NGO has based on its specific expertise or particular knowledge and existing foundations within a region. Local participation in conflict resolution efforts is fundamental so it is important to identify the impartial, professional organisations and to assist in building their capacity. In addition, it is essential to assess the sustainability of a particular programme, based on the time-scale that the NGO can commit its personnel and resources and on the available funding.

Conflict situations are complex and rife with instability and danger. Volatile political and military conditions can affect medium- to long-term strategies. As a result, short-term objectives may change and projects may be delayed. So the aim should be to define long-term strategies within a flexible shorter-term framework. Finally, the decision to engage must also include continuous risk assessment. NGOs must be aware of potential threats to themselves and the extent to which they may be endangering local partners.

Intervention in theory can come at any phase of a conflict, however it is useful to undertake *a conflict mapping exercise* using the criteria outlined above. This process helps to build a broad understanding and perspective on the issues at stake. It can help intervenors decide when, how and even whether to intervene at a particular stage, who to engage with and which tools and instruments would be most appropriate.

Stage One

UNDERSTANDING ROOT CAUSES

Too often these days, the extent of media coverage of a conflict is inversely proportional to the degree of analysis and understanding there is of causal factors and the context from which the violence has emerged. From long- and short-term historical issues, to economic trends, social and political developments, and where relevant, environmental variables, each factor offers a perspective and insight into the existing conflict. In part understanding the root causes relates to a thorough analysis of the conflict indicators mentioned in Chapter 3. The interrelationship between economic conditions and social issues must be fully appreciated.

In a multi-ethnic society, for example, where one group is wealthier than the other, a downturn in economic conditions can serve to exacerbate inter-ethnic relations. The nature and influence of political leaders needs to be assessed and understood. Their system of leadership can give a fair indication of the societal problems that may exist. In the former Yugoslavia, for example, the emergence of ultra-nationalist Serbian and Croatian leaders set the tone for the ensuing war. Long-dormant historical myths and legends were reawakened and used to demonise the Muslim population.

Finally, environmental and resource variables cannot be overlooked either. Sierra Leone, Angola, even the Burundi–Zaire border have all suffered conflict in recent years in the name of ethnicity, ideology and democracy. But without knowing that the diamond mines are at the centre of the dispute in Sierra Leone and Angola, or that through Zaire and Burundi gold smuggling is a lucrative business, it would be impossible to achieve a sustainable and long-term peace. So diamonds, gold, oil or lumber and all other economic resources must be recognised and 'mapped out'.

In addition, it is critical to elicit the reasons for violence and war from each level of society. In other words, it is important to understand why people are willing to fight, what values they fight for, whom they follow and what their beliefs are. In the current Israeli–Palestinian situation, it is Hamas which recruits and trains young suicide bombers. But who are these young men? What are their incentives and motivations? How can a message of peace and compromise reach them? If those affected by the war do not have their voices heard, their original grievances may not be addressed. This can only result in the conflict resurfacing at a later time.

IDENTIFYING ALL THE ACTORS

Secondly, the accurate identification of *all* significant actors is critical. Whether they are the visible and articulate elite and military, or the less visible, less articulate, but still influential, opinion shapers and leaders within a given society, their views and abilities to influence their communities count. In many parts of the world village or family elders still hold key positions in the local political arena. Elsewhere the military or local warlords hold influential positions. It may be difficult to fathom the various motives and agendas of each party, but it is important to try to understand them. Moreover, it is essential to be aware of the power relations that exist, as often even in the midst of a crisis there is a balance of power between groups which helps contain the levels of violence. Ignorance here could lead intervenors to tip that balance and unwittingly trigger widespread violence, as in Somalia where the UN's focus on the warlords rather than on clan leaders and groups within civil society resulted in even more trouble. Finally, concentrating only on those who shout loudest could lead the more passive elements of a community to take up arms. Listening to the grassroots is critical at all times.

IDENTIFYING FACILITATORS

Facilitators are those people who can guide and drive a communications or negotiations process forward. Facilitators should have a thorough knowledge of the conflict and strong analytical and mediation skills. They can range from 'outsider neutral' diplomats, special envoys or politicians who shuttle in and out, remaining neutral and giving objectivity and balance to events, to 'insider partials', that is local leaders, influential persons or local organisations who live with the conflict and have a strong commitment to the long-term stability of the region.

International non-governmental organisations or inter-governmental agencies can also offer medium-term support. Often they have strong grassroots ties, while also working with state officials and maintaining links with their international headquarters. So they are well placed to encourage dialogue and help diffuse tensions and misunderstandings.

Stage One: Possible Tools and Approaches

- *Peace Missions*
  IGOs, governments, NGOs and even citizens' fact-finding missions can be sent to conflict areas to define the problems.

- *Special Envoys*
  A group of experienced and credible international emissaries can be sent to speak to all parties in the conflict, exploring negotiation routes. By involving respected international figures, more attention is given to the area of conflict and more people, at both a local

and an international level show interest in participating in the resolution process.

- *Learning from Comparative Experiences*
  Experienced peacemakers can share their knowledge with local actors. By exploring the issues of conflict in an objective way, they can offer concrete examples of ways in which particular problems have been resolved in past conflicts.

Stage Two

OWNERSHIP OF THE PEACE PROCESS

The participation and empowerment of local groups, parties and associations in a peace process is fundamental. Those who have lived through a conflict must be the architects, owners and long-term stakeholders in any agreements that are reached. Peace agreements signed in Geneva or Dayton must take into account the needs and feelings of the people directly affected by the conflict. The people are the real stakeholders in the peace process and it is they who need to feel that they have been consulted and have some measure of control over negotiations which will affect them most closely.

STRATEGIC CONSTITUENCIES

By opening the peace-building process beyond the world of politicians, it would be possible to include the business, industrial, academic and other communities as well. A network of cross-sectored links involving people who have direct interest in sustaining peace could result in a series of alliances across the original social divisions. In other words, if Jewish and Arab businessmen benefit from peace, then it is in their joint interest to persuade their own constituencies to support the process.

SETTING A REALISTIC TIMETABLE

Five years of war and crimes against humanity cannot be forgotten in six months. If the purpose of a peace process is to establish security and resolve a conflict, then it is imperative that a realistic timetable is devised to cope with the reconciliation and restructuring process. Any plans must take account of a possible worsening of relations between the main parties, instability and ceasefire breakdowns. From Bosnia to Angola, the Middle East to Sierra Leone, the list of deteriorating peace processes goes on. Yet if setbacks and slowdowns are anticipated, then provisions and contingency plans can be devised to ensure the entire process does not collapse.

The tools can vary extensively, from those used by external mediators, for example, problem-solving workshops, to those organised by local communities, such as public debates and open forums for discussion. Through time, as official negotiations continue or even falter, the activities of non-state groups remains critical. For example, in Northern Ireland, following the collapse of the first ceasefire in 1996, the community-based groups and NGOs continued with their programmes of bridge-building. The popular demand for peace remains a powerful influence on the political and state officials involved in the direct talks. Ultimately, of course, they are accountable to the people they represent and must be seen to be in tune with the popular mood.

Stage Two: Possible Tools and Approaches

- *Problem-solving*
  A variety of problem-solving methods are used. One example is the promotion of informal discussions with and between disputants, or those close to them, to analyse the issues and work together to find mutually acceptable solutions. These workshops can be conducted over a period of time, giving each group a chance to express their emotions and voice their fears in a non-adversarial setting. The range of issues considered can be very broad, from tackling land dispute issues to addressing racial tension and the drawing up of legislation.

- *Training Workshops*
  The objective of these workshops is to transfer mediation and reconciliation skills to disputants, and others affected by the conflict. Each workshop can be designed to fit the needs of the participants at each stage of a conflict. For example, in Dagestan where ethnic tensions are running high, training workshops can help political and community leaders to negotiate their differences. While in Burundi, even as the conflict rages, training workshops with women's groups are helping to encourage grassroots understanding of the conflict and possible ways forward.

- *Capacity-Building*
  This is linked to the above, but also includes the provision of technical and logistical assistance for mediation efforts to the relevant actors and communities. Material assistance can range from computers, books and general office equipment, to simple paper and pen. Training in the use of computers and administration is also important.

  Capacity-building measures can also include the enhancement of public officials and civil servants' skills and abilities to administer and govern during the negotiations and post-conflict phase. Officials can be trained in leadership and management skills, the implementation of an effective taxation system, adherence to human rights and democratic values, and issues relating to corruption. By providing training at local levels, regional populations can be made to feel better represented in the national arena.

- *Peace Initiatives*
  Community-based initiatives such as 'peace zones' and 'days of peace' facilitate the provision of food supplies to certain areas and strengthen confidence-building in divided societies. These initiatives aim to galvanise local communities and villages into taking a more active role. It is also a means of bolstering people's confidence at a time when most people are desperate and can see no prospect of change.

- *Peace Conference or Citizens' Task Force*
  Citizen-based peace groups or national peace conferences can bring together different sectors of society and encourage them to formulate a peace agenda. By establishing a forum for discussion, different working groups have the opportunity to exchange ideas and develop a common agenda and agreed plan of action.

- *Linking Differences*
  One very useful means of encouraging dialogue is by providing informal settings where disputants can have a chance to relax and engage in discussion. To avoid the embarrassment of official confrontation an informal gathering could be arranged through a neutral third party, where disputants have the chance to speak openly without fear of retaliation from their own supporters or the enemy. It is part of the 'humanising' process, in which disputants are encouraged to dispel stereotypical images of each other, so that they can once again talk as ordinary people relating to each other, not as soldiers and enemies.

Stage Three

SUSTAINING THE EFFORT

In effect signing a peace agreement is the beginning of the most difficult part of peace-building. Long after the euphoria has subsided, people take stock of the death and destruction that they face. Without the means to rebuild their lives or develop an economy, the slide back into violence becomes only too easy. It is crucial, therefore, that adequate investment is dedicated to rebuilding basic infrastructures.

Many governments are willing to pledge money in support of peace, and most are keen to invest in a war-torn society in need of

road building, electricity and so forth. Yet often, as in the case of
Palestine, the money does not arrive when it is most needed. In
the occupied territories of Palestine, two years after the signing of
the Oslo agreement, little of the aid pledged to the PLO to meet
basic health, housing or nutritional needs had materialised. In
some cases money and resources have been siphoned off by corrupt
officials. During that same time, the extremist militant group
Hamas provided the necessary facilities. As a result, grassroots
support for the PLO's mediations have waned.

External political support is also important, as it helps to keep
all disputants accountable for their actions. With the world watching,
it is more difficult to break promises or retract pledges. The contrast
can be seen between Northern Ireland and the Middle East on one
hand, and Liberia and Angola on the other. While the former have
the world's political and media spotlights trained on the words and
actions of each side, in the latter, there is little external interest.
Consequently, 14 or so peace agreements were signed in Liberia
before the fighting actually stopped. Angola had elections and a
nominal peace agreement, but few Angolans live in real peace.

Stage Three: Possible Tools and Approaches

- *Economic Assistance or Political Packages*
  By drawing attention to the advantages of economic co-operation
  between regions of conflict, the opportunities for development
  and mutual benefit, disputants can be encouraged to enter into
  peace talks and discuss a more balanced political and economic
  power-sharing base.

- *Police and Military Training*
  Retraining the military and law enforcement agencies to complement
  and support peace processes is essential. Often the police and
  military are one and the same. The purpose here would be first to
  distinguish between domestic policing methods and the role of
  armed soldiers in peace-time, and to assist in the demobilisation
  and rehabilitation of soldiers into civil society. In regions of potential
  inter-state or regional violence, neighbouring governments can
  undertake a number of confidence-building measures which serve
  to build trust and mutual co-operation.

  In Central America, the Central American Security Treaty involving
  Guatemala, Costa Rica, Nicaragua, Honduras and El Salvador bans
  signatories to the treaty from supporting insurrections against
  each other and requires co-operation over drug and arms trafficking.
  Between Pakistan and India, and North and South Korea there is
  agreement to provide prior notification in case of troop manoeuvres.

Other military measures which can be taken include the professionalisation and restructuring of military forces so that previously opposing groups are integrated, thereby creating a national army rather than a factional one. Troop numbers can be reduced and emphasis can be placed on training and educating personnel to support democratic policies and reduce their role in internal repression. Furthermore the development of a socially balanced army loyal to the state can reduce the likelihood of military coups against the government, and of soldiers perpetrating or supporting ethnic conflicts.

- *Legal and Judiciary Reforms*
  The strengthening and reform of an independent judiciary is a key element in sustaining the peace effort. People must have confidence in the judiciary and the judiciary in turn must provide legal assistance and protect human rights. The judiciary can also call for the government and military to be more accountable to their constituents and provide an impartial political environment in which opposing political parties air their views.

- *Peace Monitors*
  Peace and human rights groups can monitor the safety of civilians. The development of a code of conduct for adherence to human rights and humanitarian law is one step towards introducing accountability. Special 'peace brigades' can be formed to monitor ceasefires, secure the safety of peace corridors and accompany human rights lawyers, so as to deter any attacks.

- *Human Rights Standard-setting*
  Numerous international humanitarian laws and human rights standards exist, but they are rarely invoked in internal conflicts. Campaigns stressing the importance of these laws and pressing for an international framework through which they could be implemented could help alleviate much of the current suffering. Amnesty International and Human Rights Watch are amongst the largest organisations monitoring human rights abuses by states and insurgency movements world-wide. By publicising their findings they do put pressure on governments to change their treatment of political prisoners and inform the international community of the extent of abuse that exists. They can have an enormous impact on the public's perception of a particular state, and thus also influence foreign and economic policy towards those states.

Complementary Initiatives Through Conflict Phases

In Chapter 3 we discussed the early action strategies and initiatives that different actors could undertake in a conflict situation. This complementarity and division of labour based on the comparative advantages of each sector can also be effective in initiating and generating a peace process. In other words, the efficacy of each actor at different stages of a conflict can be assessed and the knowledge gained from that evaluation can be employed to take the negotiations forward. Above, this was discussed in relation to the Norwegian initiative in the Middle East which set the stage for pre-negotiation discussions. In the case of the Mozambican peace process of 1990–92, the success of the multi-track and sequential approach is more evident.

Being in the Right Place at the Right Time – the Mozambique Peace Process

The peace talks facilitated by Sant' Egidio, the Italian government and the Archbishop of Mozambique's Beira province came at a time when the civil war had raged for 13 years. Previous attempts to end the violence had failed, as the rebels, Renamo, with heavy backing from the apartheid regime in South Africa, fought a relentless battle to overthrow the government. Aborted peace talks in 1983 had led to more vicious fighting. Regional attempts at mediation, and the involvement of the British businessman Tiny Rowland to entice the rebels and government officials to meet had failed. National church-based initiatives had also faltered. Throughout that time, using personal contacts and relations, Sant' Egidio's staff established links with Frelimo, the Italian government and the Vatican. Moreover, as providers of humanitarian aid through the church network, Sant' Egidio was able to develop a network of associates throughout the country. Its relations with Renamo also began during the height of the conflict, when Sant' Egidio was able to negotiate the release of hostages and provide humanitarian aid to Renamo-controlled territories. So, long before the talks process began, in the pre-negotiations phase, Sant' Egidio had worked towards building trust and confidence with both parties.

Finally, in 1990, the two sides agreed to talk, and so earnest negotiations began. Despite numerous disagreements, the two parties finally settled on restricting the level of mediation and intervention during the talks. The UN, the US, the Portuguese government, various European and regional southern African states were consulted as observers but were not permitted to mediate between the two sides. Even when Renamo requested UN and US intervention, the request was denied, for it was agreed between all parties concerned that the additional intervention and assistance would come in the aftermath of a peace agreement.

The process continued for two years, at times proceeding rapidly, while at other times at risk of complete failure. However, throughout this time, regional initiatives were also being undertaken. Moreover, the US and other donor countries were preparing the ground for the provision of technical and financial aid for reconstruction. Meanwhile the UN was setting a timetable for the deployment of peacekeepers, decommissioning of arms and demobilisation, and elections.

By October 1992, the Rome talks were fused together with regional discussions. All sides met for the final peace-signing ceremony. From then on Sant' Egidio stepped back from the arena, to allow others to continue the process. In essence, therefore, Sant' Egidio's comparative advantage was during the pre-negotiations and negotiations phases, when trust-building and creating spaces for discussion and dialogue was critical. Once agreements were reached and the process entered into an implementation phase, it was the UN and donor governments who were best placed to assist. The success of each, however, depended on the other. Of course, each conflict is unique, as are the exact methods of resolving it. It is most unlikely, for example, that the role of Sant' Egidio can be imitated elsewhere. But the principle of employing different individuals and organisations committed to long-term peace is one which needs to be more widely accepted and more assiduously promoted.

Evaluations and Effectiveness

Yet in this step-by-step approach to peace how is it possible to judge the efficacy of any specific tool or initiative? How can it be known whether a peace conference, experience-sharing event or a series of conflict resolution training workshops had any impact? In Mozambique how can we assess to what extent, if at all, the grassroots church-based activities were instrumental in bringing about the final peace agreements? It is true that those initiatives faltered in bringing about negotiations, but perhaps a number of critical issues were raised which contributed to the final solution.

The means of evaluation and testing of most initiatives, whether in the early preventive stages of conflict or in the height of violence, is a difficult task. But rigorous evaluation is imperative if these initiatives and those involved as practitioners in the field are to gain credibility and legitimacy. Moreover, given the harsh economic realities under which communities live in times of conflict, it is often difficult to justify spending funds on intangible problem-solving workshops instead of on more tangible goods, such as books for children or blankets in the winter. An evaluation process also helps to improve tools and projects. Finally, given the volatility of conflict conditions, some initiatives may inadvertently serve to exacerbate a situation. Without a means of judging and assessing them, these issues may not be so apparent.

One approach to measure the effectiveness of any initiative would be to assess it against its influence on the outcome of a conflict.[34] It is necessary to hypothesise about possible worst-case scenarios or violent outcomes of a situation, and consider the likelihood of such an outcome if first, the initiative was not taken, or second, if the initiative had been taken at a different time. Another approach would be to assess the impact of any action against the wider context or factors which are thought to be the causes of the conflict.

An alternative approach would be to measure the effectiveness of one action against alternative approaches. So, if the objective is to stimulate public interest and participation in the prevention or resolution of a conflict, the effectiveness of a series of public debates could be measured against, for example, that of a press or media campaign. Quantitative comparisons can be made in terms of the costs of each approach. But in terms of the benefits, the comparisons must be qualitative.

Conclusion

The practice of diplomacy or of inter-state relations has come a long way since the days of the ancient Greeks or Renaissance Italians. With unimagined levels of global communication, travel and interdependence, states are not only becoming accountable to each other, but also to members of civil society across the world. This civil society or loose and disparate network of community and citizen-based groups is increasingly more active in the area of peacemaking, conflict prevention and resolution. Given the complexity and uniqueness of each conflict situation, it is important to have such complementary forces working in unison to bring peace.

Countless obstacles still exist. Like the UN, NGOs are accused of lacking neutrality and impartiality. They too can be demonised by one or both sides in a conflict. To some extent, they still face the problem of legitimacy. They need to have a clearer mandate on how, when and with whose consent they can legitimately intervene in conflict situations. To this end their relationships with intergovernmental organisations must be clarified and based on a greater degree of trust and transparency.

Confidentiality is another major concern for NGOs. The nature of the work is confidential and low-profile. Yet often donors, governments and other interested parties request information about their progress. But precisely because there are long-term commitments and the progress made is fragile, there is a reluctance to proclaim short-term successes too quickly. To ensure their own credibility NGOs (and other mediators) must at all times recognise that it is the disputants and civilian populations who own and are responsible for carrying a peace process forward.

Finally, NGOs must be aware of the overtly political nature of the field. Any form of intervention is an attempt at transforming power relations and in internal conflicts such interventions can have a profound impact. So, by intervening they are undertaking a major responsibility. It is therefore essential that NGOs develop a stringent code of conduct by which they operate and through which they can protect their non-partisan position.

At a theoretical level these issues are readily acknowledged. In practice, given the volatility of conflict situations, the focus and objectives of third party mediators can get lost. The answers will never be set and available in a small handbook. However, by exchanging experiences and co-ordinating their efforts, those involved in any form of diplomacy or intervention can help develop that code of conduct and a menu of options, which could form the basis of future conflict resolution and prevention activities.

CHAPTER 5

Ending Warfare, Creating Accountability

The real experience of war is not the shelling and so on, those are just moments, though they are the ones you see on TV. War is what happens afterwards, the years of suffering hopelessly with a disabled husband and no money, or struggling to rebuild when all your property has been destroyed.

(Arms to Fight, Arms to Protect, *1995*)[1]

Introduction

As one millennium draws to a close and another approaches, there are those who question humanity's capacity to build a peaceful future for itself. The twentieth century has witnessed to two world wars and an ignominious series of civil wars, genocide and ethnocides on an unprecedented scale. Will the twenty-first century produce more of the same, or will it offer greater opportunities for managing and resolving conflicts more peacefully?

This book has argued that given a better understanding of the nature and causes of contemporary conflicts, peace is possible. Already we are seeing a decline in the number of wars being fought world-wide and the spread of democracy is bringing with it the instruments and mechanisms for the peaceful resolution of conflicts. There are still many obstacles to be overcome. The threat of a global nuclear war may be receding, but the risk of the proliferation of weapons of mass destruction is increasing. Pressure on scarce resources, land and water may yet provoke untold violence and the rise of religious extremism and nationalism is an ever-present threat to global security.

Much can be done, however, to mitigate these threats and prevent these conflicts from breaking out. In Chapter 3, we examined the importance of an effective early warning system to identify potential crises, and in Chapter 4, we explored ways in which non-state actors and citizen groups could participate in the processes of conflict transformation. In this final chapter, we discuss strategies for war termination and the need for a new series of standards and norms for conduct in internal conflicts. In doing so, we highlight the measures needed, not only to make the perpetrators of war more

138

accountable to the international community, but to make the practice of warfare increasingly difficult in the future.

Just as the escalation towards armed conflict progresses through different stages of intense hostility, so too the restoration of peace occurs through a gradual de-escalation process. To be successful, it must be accompanied by concrete measures which meet the long-term needs of both the disputants and the wider population. The dangers of misunderstanding, distrust, further polarisation and an eventual return to armed conflict are acute, particularly in the early stages. From Northern Ireland to Angola, from Liberia[2] to Bosnia,[3] it has become clear that breaking peace agreements is far easier than sustaining them.

Strategies for War Termination

From our discussions in the previous chapters it is evident that ending civil wars is a complex and difficult task. Previous research in this area indicates that not only are civil wars more difficult to settle than inter-state wars, but that, when they come, the settlements themselves are more fragile. Historically, negotiated solutions to such wars have been rare. Since 1800 only one third of all civil wars have ended through negotiations. Since 1945 that ratio stands at 25 per cent.[4] Although the Ethiopian war and the more recent conflict in the former Zaire ended through military solutions, compromise solutions are becoming more prevalent. Liberia, El Salvador and Guatemala are amongst the conflicts terminated through negotiations in recent years.

There are no set patterns or models applicable to every conflict. But one process that can be used is to identify potential targets for negotiations. By aiming to understand and unveil the belligerents' incentives for continued fighting, their disincentives for compromise and the structural features of the conflict, third party mediators can develop specific strategies for initiating negotiations. In his book *Ending Civil Wars*, Charles King identifies several key factors.[5]

- Leadership
- Making War Unprofitable
- Reducing Asymmetry
- Guaranteeing Security

Leadership

The issue of leadership is amongst the biggest obstacles to be overcome by third party mediators. Leaders, be they heads of state or of guerrilla movements, can be uncooperative and recalcitrant. Opponents may often demand the removal of a leader before agreeing to enter into negotiations. Yet few leaders are willing to step down from power. As a result neither side is willing to engage in power-sharing agreements. Both sides may agree to participate in democratic elections, but if the results are disappointing to one side, its likelihood of reneging on the original agreement increases.

To address this problem, King argues that a change in leadership, whether through death or other means, can create opportunities for negotiation. Indeed, such an event does often provoke a period of assessment and reflection on the conflict situation. The examples of Mozambique in 1986, and Chechnya and Sierra Leone in 1996, suggest that leadership changes can have a positive effect on the search for a solution. Of course, the opposite can also hold true, especially if a vacuum at the top results in a power struggle or if a conciliatory leader is toppled by more extremist factions. But under certain conditions a change of leadership can increase the chances for negotiations. These include:

- If the incumbent leader is a key obstacle to negotiations.
- If successors are united in their desire for peace.
- If the successor is keen to distance him/herself from the policies of his/her predecessors.

Making War Unprofitable

Reducing the profitability of war can be a major blow to belligerents. War often spawns its own economy. It can mean good business for governments and for insurgency movements, particularly since criminality is now a significant component in many contemporary conflicts. It is important that the international community responds to this disturbing new phenomenon by freezing the bank accounts and seizing the assets of those suspected of involvement in the conflict. Restricting a group's ability to purchase weapons can be instrumental in forcing it to the negotiating table.

Reducing Asymmetry

This policy can be effective, too, in reducing the imbalances between the warring groups and creating a 'level playing field'. External powers are often in a strong position to influence one or both sides' capacity to wage war by denying them aid, access to weapons or money, and refusing to offer safe havens to the fighters. There is no doubt that the end of the Cold War was a significant factor in the resolution of the Mozambique conflict. In Latin America also the El Salvador peace agreement of 1992 was hastened by the withdrawal of Soviet and Cuban aid. The loss of support can be a major equaliser in internal conflicts.

Although neutralising one side's physical superiority can be a useful first step, it does not address the problem of equal legitimacy between opposing sides in a conflict. Frequently, indigenous communities have no political channels through which to voice their grievances and state their demands. Without a recognised political voice, they are at risk of being ignored. To counteract this, potential mediators can offer technical assistance and facilitate the process of communication in a number of ways. In relation to claims over land, the example below offers one solution.

Mapping Land and Settling Claims of Ownership[6]

In northern Honduras, cattle ranchers, loggers and landless peasant farmers encroached on Indian homelands. With no support from the state or judiciary, Indian leaders and cultural activists undertook their own mapping exercise. By helping Indians to create detailed records of their homelands, they ensured that the authorities could not ignore their existence.

The mapping process included several workshops, land use surveys and finally a national-level forum to present the results. At the first workshop, the area of land in question was divided into zones of manageable size. Indigenous surveyors and co-ordinators with intimate knowledge of the region were chosen to develop questionnaires about land use and agree procedures for administering the surveys and mapping the land-use areas.

A subsequent census determined the land used for farming, hunting, fishing, gathering medicinal plants and materials for houses, canoes and crafts and other activities. Following workshops and meetings with cartographers the information was checked against existing maps and the villages involved, and new maps were drawn up.

Mapping indigenous homelands debunked the myth that these lands were uninhabited. Areas of land previously viewed by the authorities as 'degraded' (forest, savanna and wetland) were found to conform to areas actively occupied by native Americans. The political momentum created by the process of land mapping raised the regional awareness of the Indians, showing them the common ground they shared with other indigenous peoples, and it empowered them to pursue legal protection of their homelands. This project was replicated with success in Panama.

Guaranteeing Security

As King suggests, the absence of objective and credible security guarantees is a critical issue for all parties in a conflict.[7] Typically, belligerents rely on their own fighting power for security, so they are reluctant to disarm and leave themselves vulnerable to possible attack. This security dilemma can be the single most potent factor in the success or failure of a peace settlement.

At the heart of this dilemma is the problem of timing. Insurgents are usually unwilling to disarm or even agree to a ceasefire for fear of being attacked by the government or having their interests overlooked. Governments typically are unwilling to engage in talks or political reform unless there is a ceasefire and disarmament. In Northern Ireland, the disagreement over the decommissioning of arms led to the breakdown of the first ceasefire agreement in early 1996. In Sierra Leone, disagreement over the role of the mercenary group, Executive Outcomes, fighting on the government's side, and the RUF/SL guerrillas resulted in months of delay over the signing of the first fateful peace declaration in 1996.

But the reluctance to disarm is not simply based on a collective fear of attack. For many combatants left disillusioned or traumatised by years of war, the ownership of a weapon is integral to their survival. The skills acquired in warfare bear little relevance to civilian life, leaving only banditry and criminality as avenues for income-generation. With a gun, they have access to food and material goods; without one, they are as vulnerable as other members of society.

Moreover, the actual process of disarmament is complicated by the nature of the weapons that are used. Light, cheap, easily hidden and transported, it is virtually impossible to know what quantity of arms exist in war-torn countries, so attempting to disarm the population forcibly is often impossible. It is important, therefore, to devise a strategy which not only addresses the broader issues of security, but also offers the right incentives for combatants to disarm willingly.

Demobilising and Reintegrating Eritrean fighters[8]

When the war finally ended in Eritrea, there were an estimated 100,000 former guerrilla fighters, of the EPLF. In 1993, the first group of fighters, including 27,000 of the youngest soldiers, was demobilised. One year later, the demobilisation of veteran fighters began. Having spent 15–18 years fighting for liberation, these men had no property and minimal experience of surviving in a civilian market economy. But they were disciplined, hard-working and willing to take on the challenge of survival anew.

The Agency for Co-operation and Research in Development (ACORD) and the Eritrean Relief and Rehabilitation Agency (ERRA-Mitias) developed a programme of brick- and tile-making targeting the ex-fighters, both men and women. Former combatants were organised into production teams which then operated as independent economic units. The bricks and tiles they made supplied other building projects run by ACORD and ERRA-Mitias (e.g. shelter construction and sanitation projects). The overall aim of the programme was to allow reintegration of the ex-fighters to take place by giving them a valid economic role and the ability to become self-sufficient. For the women the programme also offered a socially acceptable activity as they re-entered civilian life.

The fighters were trained in the practical and managerial skills of running a business. To ensure local self-sufficiency, the machines used were also produced locally. In all, 40 production teams were established.

This process can be encouraged through a synchronised programme of demobilisation, combining reforms in state military structures with reintegration programmes. Such programmes generally involve cash compensation, training or a means of generating income for combatants, their families and other displaced people. Quite often psychological counselling is needed to cope with the immense changes that civilian life brings. Moreover, if these programmes are accompanied by political reform, the chances of a prolonged deadlock can be reduced.

Buy-back Schemes in Haiti and Nicaragua[9]

During its involvement in the multinational force in *Haiti*, the US Army conducted a gun buy-back programme. At first mobile units were set up, protected by US troops. Payments were made for functional weapons; those without the firing pin were confiscated. Between September 1994 and March 1995, 33,000 weapons and munitions were collected at a cost of almost US$ 2 million. The prices paid varied between $ 100 and $ 600 according to weapon type. But the range included machine guns, assault rifles, CS gas grenades, a variety of pistols, flare guns and even several tanks. On collection they were examined. Those in good condition were recycled and used for training the Haitian police, those with historical value were classified as museum pieces and the remainder were destroyed.

In *Nicaragua*, despite the government's reintegration programme, many ex-fighters rearmed from hidden arms caches. So a buy-back programme was set up in 1991. The average paid for a weapon was $100 in cash, and a further $100 worth of food. The Italian government sponsored a micro-enterprise, offering $300–500 to each participant as seed money. In addition, payments were made for information on arms caches and groups that had rearmed. The system was flexible, allowing groups to sell their arms in exchange for food, cash and construction material that they needed. In total the operation cost $6 million and succeeded in destroying over 500,000 weapons and munitions. The weapons were burnt in a big pit in a large public space. It was thought to be both cost-effective and psychologically a positive social act.

Generating Accountability

In part the challenge facing the international community is to develop criteria which can make war and armed conflict culturally and globally unacceptable. To some extent this has already happened. The fact that war is no longer glorified, that governments are under pressure not to send young men to die in foreign lands, that complex intergovernmental structures such as the EU and the UN actually exist is a tribute to those who in witnessing the horrors of warfare, declared 'never again', and took concrete steps in that direction. The issue now is to take those measures further in relation to the wars that we see today.

The challenges faced by the international community today are manifold. First, there is a need to develop a framework and a series of norms and standards which would encourage parties to talk before violence breaks out (similar to the OSCE High Commissioner on National Minorities). Second, there is a need to ensure that if violence does break out, the instruments and approaches needed to prevent the escalation of the conflict also exist. Third, mechanisms are needed to ensure that all belligerents, state and *non-state actors* fulfil their obligations in upholding international human rights and humanitarian laws.

In terms of human rights violations legislation, state obligation and accountability have progressed quite considerably. By being signatories to international conventions and protocols, states are liable to be monitored. Institutions such as the Human Rights Commission, Amnesty International and Human Rights Watch have brought greater visibility and accountability to the actions of states. This is not to say that states no longer commit atrocities, but they can be held accountable to international law. Their statements can be publicly contested at the Human Rights Commission and confirmed or discredited through the publication of reports.

Bringing accountability to the actions of non-state groups is more difficult at present. But interesting progress is being made in making non-state actors and guerrilla movements acknowledge and occasionally adhere to international laws. Amnesty International and Human Rights Watch also monitor the violations of human rights by non-state groups, and have denounced their lack of adherence to international laws. Amongst such groups, the Taliban in Afghanistan, not known for their respect of international human rights or humanitarian standards, have submitted complaints regarding the mistreatment of their fighters to the International Red Cross. In Sierra Leone and Sri Lanka, the RUF/SL and LTTE are taking human rights issues more seriously. They realise that a universal condemnation of their actions serves to undermine their position in the international arena and their ambitions to become viable political entities. So there is some willingness to adhere to certain norms. Furthermore, there is better international co-operation between security agencies tracking criminal activities and armed groups. Surveillance of insurgency groups and greater international agreement on what constitutes terrorism is generating a less hospitable environment for transnational actors involved in violent armed conflict.

As more attention focuses on the problems associated with internal conflict, more systematic procedures are also being developed to tackle these issues. Following in the footsteps of the landmine campaign, a series of other initiatives listed below are also being expanded.

- Addressing impunity
- Controlling the spread of small arms
- Protection of children in war
- Promoting the application of international humanitarian laws to internal armed conflict
- Strengthening civil society and building local capacities towards conflict prevention

Addressing Impunity

Indiscriminate killings, rape, torture and unjustified imprisonment – impunity means the perpetrators of these acts literally 'get away' with it. They are never judged or punished. When war ends, or an oppressive regime is finally toppled, many people, particularly the victimised, say that there can be no peace or reconciliation without justice. They want to see the perpetrators prosecuted. Within the context of a stable liberal democratic state, this call for justice is by and large heeded. The judiciary acts independently, laws are implemented and violators are punished accordingly. But in the context of a war-torn society, or one which has experienced decades of oppression and structural violence, administering justice is fraught with difficulty.

Often the state has no resources to support war crimes tribunals. In Rwanda, apart from the flawed judicial system, the sheer numbers waiting to be tried are an unmanageable weight on the government's shoulders. There are just a handful of experienced lawyers in the country. International resources and aid have been provided for the training of prosecutors, but they still lack the necessary legal expertise to undertake free and fair trials. Furthermore, given that most of the real leaders and perpetrators of the genocide fled the country, many of those being held are either innocent or themselves victims of the tide of events. The trials conducted in Kigali and Arusha are neither effective nor reconciliatory. Witnesses are customarily threatened or assassinated. Since no real effort has been made to reform the judiciary itself, resentment against the current Tutsi-dominated government from the majority Hutu population has risen once again.

From Bosnia and Rwanda to Guatemala and South Africa, impunity has been the cause of intense debate. It can breed vengeance and further violence. Denying that the military or security services in Guatemala or South Africa tortured and killed thousands of people can be seen as condoning their actions and placing them above the law. Inequality in the eyes of the law can, in turn, compromise the entire basis of democracy in a country. However, resurrecting past misdeeds strengthens animosities and hampers reconciliation efforts. Hand-picking individuals and boxing villains, heroes and victims in simple categories obscures the wider structural factors which were at fault.[10]

TRUTH COMMISSIONS

In searching for the balance between retribution and justice on one hand, and 'forgetfulness' and denial on the other, throughout Latin America, *truth* has become the focal point. 'Truth commissions' or commissions of inquiry have been established in Chile, Brazil, El Salvador, Argentina and elsewhere. Their primary objective is to investigate and, more importantly, *acknowledge* the political killings, torture and human rights abuses committed by previous regimes. In some instances, amnesty laws were passed making members of the past regime exempt from prosecution, but more willing to talk.

Listening to a member of the secret police describe how one's son or daughter was killed, then watching him walk away to freedom is neither fair nor easy. But even for the relatives of the victims, it is often the admittance of responsibility, the final confirmation of what really happened and the chance to recover the bodies of the dead which are of real significance psychologically. In South Africa the admittance by two security servicemen of their role in the death of Steve Biko had a tremendously positive impact on the process of trust-building between the black and white communities. Ideally everyone should have access to justice, but given the often bleak realities, establishing truth commissions has proved to be a worthwhile compromise.

But truth commissions are not the long-term solution to the problems of justice. There is a need to tackle the profound structural elements which perpetuate corruption and impunity amongst state or official bodies. Focusing attention on education and the development of new standards of behaviour for the military or police forces can be more effective than punishing a few. Similarly, empowering the judiciary to become independent of political control is itself a fundamental step towards ensuring freedom and security for society at large.

Helping to Develop an Independent Judiciary[11]

Cambodia: The Khmer Rouge, when in power, systematically massacred all judges and lawyers. As a result what judiciary that existed was run by individuals with no legal training and even less independence. In May 1993, following democratic elections, emphasis was given to the need for institution-building and the reconstruction of democratic social structures. The Swiss-based Centre for the Independence of Judges and Lawyers (CIJL) ran a three-week seminar on 'Judicial Functions and Independence' in Cambodia. Fifty-six judges and members of the Supreme Court and Court of Appeal participated. During the three-week period, prominent international lawyers and judges were invited to lead the seminar. A wide range of criminal, civil and constitutional laws and procedures were studied and explored in relation to Cambodian traditions and culture. The issue of independence was explored and in general the legal education of the participants was furthered.

As a *preliminary step* towards the development of an independent judiciary, the seminar series was a success. Establishing a fully independent and strong system will take much longer, and will require that elusive political stability.

PERMANENT INTERNATIONAL CRIMINAL COURT

In addition to developing independent state judiciaries, the experiences of the Bosnian and Rwandan war crimes tribunals has generated a major campaign for the creation of a permanent international criminal court. Amnesty International, the ICRC, Earthaction and a host of other organisations are calling for an end to the ad hoc creation of these tribunals, arguing that the existing systems are expensive and inefficient.[12]

The campaigners argue that a permanent international criminal court (ICC) would strengthen the UN's capability to uphold international security and give it greater powers to address internal conflicts. The movement is proving effective in its lobbying of the UN and in influencing the structure and function of the court.

Amongst the major issues being debated is that the court should have the right to hold *individuals* accountable for their violations of international laws, including war crimes, crimes against humanity and genocide.[13] Moreover, it is hoped that an ICC would accept the information provided by individuals, NGOs or governments, in addition to the court's own prosecuting body for bringing cases against any person, group or state engaged in serious international crimes. Another major issue on the campaign's agenda is to ensure that the court has jurisdiction to prosecute those guilty of committing atrocities in *non-international* armed conflict. Thus perpetrators of violence in internal conflicts could be charged in the international arena.

Amnesty International's Basic Principles Concerning the International Criminal Court[14]

- States have the primary responsibility of bringing those responsible for serious crimes under international law to justice, but the International Criminal Court must be able to act as an effective complement to states when they are unable or unwilling to fulfil their duty.

- The court must have the power to determine whether to exercise its concurrent jurisdiction in such cases.

- The court should have jurisdiction over the three core crimes of genocide, other crimes against humanity and serious violations of humanitarian law applicable to international and *non-international* armed conflict.

- The court should have inherent (automatic) universal jurisdiction over the core crimes under international law, so that it can exercise concurrent jurisdiction with respect to each *state party* in appropriate circumstances.

- Each of the core crimes and applicable defences should be clearly defined.

- Inadmissable defences under international law, such as superior orders, should be excluded.

- Penalties must be clearly stated. The death penalty should be excluded.

- The prosecutor should be able to initiate investigations in any case where the court has jurisdiction, even in the absence of referral by the Security Council or a state complaint, *based on information from any source* and to submit an indictment to the court.

- The statute of the court should permit the Security Council to submit to it situations involving threats to or breaches of, international peace and security and acts of aggression, but not individual cases. The statute should not, however, permit the Security Council to prevent the investigation and prosecution of cases involving such situations.

There is much controversy, numerous obstacles and a host of procedural and practical issues which need to be tackled before such a court became operational. But again the effectiveness of the global coalition was made evident when in 1997 Kofi Annan, the UN Secretary General, declared his support for the court by stating;

> There can be no global justice unless the worst crimes are subject to the law ... The establishment of an international criminal court will ensure that humanity's response will be swift and just ... The General Assembly has decided to convene a conference ... in 1998 to adopt a convention on the establishment of an international criminal court ...[15]

Controlling the Spread of Arms

In parallel to the legislative developments, it is also important to address practical issues such as the proliferation of small arms and trends towards the increasing militarisation of many societies. The success of the landmines campaign in mobilising the support of people and organisations from around the world provides a striking example of what can be achieved when enough pressure can be brought to bear on governments.

LANDMINES
The 1997 Nobel Prize award to the International Campaign to Ban Landmines was a major symbolic endorsement of the campaign's objectives. It began as a small campaign in the 1980s, but has expanded into a global network of non-governmental agencies, engineering experts, mine specialists, local people in each country and, increasingly, state agencies and intergovernmental organisations. Their primary objective was to achieve a comprehensive world-wide ban on the production, sale and distribution of landmines. This vision came that much closer to being realised in November 1997 when 120 nations ratified a treaty banning the production, sale and use of landmines. Unfortunately, the states most responsible for the manufacture of these mines, the USA, China and Russia, refused to sign the treaty. Nevertheless, the campaign has brought the issue of landmines to the very forefront of inter-

national affairs. As a result, de-mining technology has improved considerably and more resources are now being directed towards de-mining some of the 120 million mines already laid.

SMALL ARMS

In theory, a campaign to restrict the trade in small arms – defined as light, portable weapons – should have a better chance of success than a landmine ban. Most governments already oppose the illicit trade which is responsible for arming criminals and insurgent groups, and many also favour a code of conduct regulating which countries are deemed 'responsible' enough to buy weapons on the open market. For its part, the UN has already implemented a number of measures designed to restrict the flow of arms, but these have merely illustrated the difficulty of monitoring such flows. The importance of cutting off the supply of light weapons, however, cannot be underestimated. Their prevalence makes them responsible for much of the killing around the world and their easy availability ensures that societies are plagued by violence long after the conflict itself has ended. A curb on the illicit arms trade would restrict the ability of rebel groups to wage war, whilst a restrictive code of conduct on the legal trade would limit the capacity of governments to misuse weapons for internal repression. Taken together, these two measures would reduce the likelihood of war and help bring combatants to the negotiating table.

The movement to secure a global ban on the sale of weapons to repressive or aggressive regimes has gathered pace following the success of the landmines campaign. The proposed code of conduct will establish four eligibility criteria which must be met by governments seeking to purchase weapons:

- democratic form of government
- respect for internationally recognised norms of human rights
- non-aggression against neighbouring states
- participation in the UN Register of Conventional Arms

The success of such a code of conduct will, of course, depend heavily on the number of countries which sign up to it. It is little use the EU introducing restrictions (as it has pledged to do) if the US, Russia and China do not. For the code to have any real effect, it will need to be truly global and implemented in conjunction with a range of other measures. For the difficulty lies not so much in curbing the licit arms trade but in restricting the availability of weapons on the black market. At present, it is all but impossible to track the flow of arms and there is no co-ordinated system for determining the source of the weapons. These difficulties are further exacerbated by the sheer quantity of arms in the world today. This is largely a legacy of the Cold War during which the superpowers flooded the developing world with a surfeit of weapons of all kinds. It would not be unusual, for example, to discover an African guerrilla using an American-made gun left over from the Vietnam War.

In response to growing concern over the scale of the problem, a number of NGOs involved in conflict resolution organised a series of conferences to debate the issues with government officials, members of the military and representatives from academic institutions and civil society organisations from around the world. The result of these discussions was a number of recommendations designed to enhance security in conflict-prone areas and contribute to the removal of weapons from society. Of the 17 recommendations made at the conferences, the most important are summarised below:

- Support should be provided for disarmament programmes, the demobilisation of soldiers and capacity building.
- Governments, NGOs and donors should develop regional programmes to destroy weapons deemed to be excessive.
- Priority should be given to investment in education programmes to reverse the culture of weapons possession.
- All states, without exception, should adhere to the standards of international human rights conventions.
- Producer countries should adopt and implement codes of conduct for the responsible export of weapons.
- All light weapons and ammunition should be registered at the point of production.
- Measures should be taken at national, regional and international levels to control illicit weapons flows as well as to enhance transparency and accountability.

Nothing less than the future stability of many parts of the developing world depends upon the successful and effective implementation of these and other measures. The battle against landmines is being won, but the fight to contain and restrict the spread of light weapons will be even more important in eliminating conflict throughout the world.

The Protection of Children in War

Children and particularly child soldiers throughout the world suffer profound traumas in war-time. Many of the children are trained from a very early age to take commands, kill and maim. They may have no social skills or any education whatsoever. As mentioned in Chapter 2, often they are orphans whose only family life is found in the guerrilla forces. Disbanding these units means taking away their only source of security and identity.

José

The guerrillas gave José a rifle and told him to shoot his father. At first José refused to do so and the guerrillas began to cut off his fingers with a machete. He lost four fingers before, in desperation, he shot his father.

The guerrillas then forced him to join them as soldiers.[16]

In instances where children were abducted by guerrillas or armies and forced to commit atrocities in their own villages or against their own relatives, the return to family life can be disturbing for everyone. Increasingly in West Africa and Asia child soldiers are deliberately forced into drug addiction. They suffer profound emotional and psychological problems for which there is no easy remedy. These children require long-term care and education, which is rarely available. Furthermore, given the fact that few states or even guerrilla groups willingly admit to using child soldiers, it is difficult to gain access to them at all.

The tragedy of children in war was brought to the world's attention in 1995 by the Machal Report on *The Impact of Conflict on Children* for the UN.[17] It has led to international condemnation of the abuse of children in war and prompted a new wave of global activism regarding the protection of children from conflict.

The Impact of Conflict on Children: Summary of Recommendations[18]

- The recruitment of children into conflict can be minimised if local communities, NGOs, church groups and civil society in general co-ordinate their efforts in condemning the recruiters and pressing the authorities for the release of under-age soldiers.

- Early documentation of missing children can be effective in tracing them.

- NGOs and humanitarian agencies working in close proximity with insurgency groups areas can use their influence to discourage the recruitment of children.

- Building on the efforts of the Committee of the Rights of a Child, the Society of Friends (Quakers), UNICEF, UNHCR, the ICRC and IFRC (International Federation of Red Cross and Red Crescent Societies), a global campaign should be launched aimed at eradicating the participation of children under the age of 18 in armed forces.

- The media should be encouraged to expose the use of child soldiers.

- UN agencies should use their influence in quiet diplomacy to encourage the immediate demobilisation of child soldiers.

- All peace agreements should include specific measures for demobilising and reintegrating children back into society.

- Refugee children, or those internally displaced, should be returned to the care of their extended families as soon as possible. Specific provisions should be made available for their care and for tracing their immediate families.

- Humanitarian agencies and UN bodies should ensure the provision of special reproductive health needs especially for women and girls who have suffered sexual violations.

- To ensure the protection of children, UN agencies should work more collaboratively with ICRC and the International Labour Organisation.

- Civil society organisations helping women to sustain and protect children should be supported and developed.

- New networks of collaboration at local, national, regional and international levels should be encouraged to generate an environment for child rights activities and projects.

Promoting the Application of International Humanitarian Laws to Internal Armed Conflict

Well aware of the excesses and terrible devastation that civil war can bring, the International Committee for the Red Cross (ICRC) and Médecins Sans Frontières (MSF) have been great advocates in publicising the need to strengthen and uphold international humanitarian laws in internal conflicts. In 1989 the ICRC took steps to strengthen and expand international humanitarian legislation to incorporate internal conflicts as well. Under the auspices of the International Institute of Humanitarian Law, existing provisions regarding the conduct of hostilities in non-international armed conflicts were examined and a series of recommendations reached. In April 1990, the recommendations were approved and the 'Declaration on the Rules of International Humanitarian Law Governing the Conduct of Hostilities in Non-international Armed Conflict' was published.[19]

The rules covered two principal issues: the protection of civilians and non-combatants, and prohibition and restriction on the use of certain weapons. Civilian populations must be given immunity, must not be subjected to unnecessary injury and must be distinguished from combatants. Medical and religious personnel and units should be given protection. Civilian dwellings and objects and areas which are necessary for their survival should not be removed or destroyed. With regard to weaponry, the rules clearly state that chemical and bacteriological weapons are prohibited. 'Dumdum' bullets and other devices that explode on contact are forbidden. Poison, mines, booby-traps and other incendiary devices are also prohibited.

Much needs to be done to develop an effective means of monitoring adherence to these laws. The legislation, although signed by governments, requires a long period of time to be effectively enforced. Moreover, although in theory the laws apply to violence perpetrated by militia groups and insurgency movements, in practice non-state groups still face few if any restrictions. More measures are needed to make these groups accountable to the international community as well, something which can best be done through the creation of a permanent international court in which all violators can be brought to justice.

Strengthening Civil Society and Building Local Capacities towards Conflict Prevention

Finally, the development and continuing growth of a new network of international organisations and local community groups working towards the strengthening of civil society and the establishment of conflict resolution institutions cannot be overlooked.

Ernest Gellner defined civil society as

> the set of diverse non-governmental institutions which is strong enough to counterbalance the state and, while not preventing the state from fulfilling its role of keeper of peace and arbitrator between major interests, can nevertheless prevent it dominating and atomising the rest of society ... *Civil society – helps to clarify social norms in a way that democracy or system of one man one vote doesn't – because whereas democracy assumes that consent is better than coercion, civil society allows for a plurality of social groupings.*[20]

In other words, where religious, racial or tribal affiliations or ideologies such as communism or fascism, monitor, control or oppress an individual's thoughts, words and actions, there cannot be a strong civil society. Across Africa, Asia and Latin America the range of new conflict resolution groups and institutions which have emerged are expanding the breadth of citizen-based action. Their objectives are to create alternative means of dispute resolution in society. As mentioned in Chapter 3, many are working towards developing regional networks for conflict early warning. The numerous training and capacity-building programmes that have been devised are encouraging citizens' and grassroots groups to prevent and mitigate violence and armed conflict. In societies that are increasingly complex and multi-ethnic, they are working to enable plurality to flourish.

The importance of a global civil society has been further endorsed by The Hague Peace Conference. Since the first international peace conference at The Hague in 1899, the group has been at the forefront of developing mechanisms for building lasting world peace. It has initiated the development of international and humanitarian laws. Throughout the twentieth century the conference has made significant contributions to the creation of existing global organisations. Consequently it enjoys long standing support from governments world-wide.

In 1999 in celebration of its centenary, The Hague is holding a global conference to develop new strategies for the reduction and peaceful resolution of conflicts. The conference aims to address a comprehensive series of conflict-related issues from disarmament, to the expansion of humanitarian laws, the strengthening of civic groups and future strategies for conflict prevention world-wide. An estimated 10,000 participants from a wide cross-section of nations, governments and non-governmental groups are expected to attend. It will herald a new era in state and non-state co-operation, and in so doing will set a new charter and common global agenda for building peace in the next century.[21]

Waging War: The Less Attractive Alternative

Eliminating the scourge of internal wars will not happen overnight. But despite the threats that exist in the world today, the possibility of confining warfare to the history books is no longer an unattainable goal. There is also a growing sense of optimism about the future. Until now our assumption has been that war would not go away. This assumption has altered profoundly in recent years. The number of serious internal conflicts world-wide has declined steadily over the past two years. Without superpower support and geopolitics at play, the new conflicts and wars erupting onto the world scene today are smaller in scope than the proxy wars of the Cold War years. Or as Nicholas Berry suggests in *War and the Red Cross*:

> today's wars are vulnerable to intervention. They are small wars, unsupported by superpower patrons. Inject members of the international community into these wars as non-partisan third parties, and these rag-tag wars can be overwhelmed and made dysfunctional. They can be sabotaged. The third parties would have, in most cases, enough capabilities to upset the power relations between the warring parties and prevent victory by one side, to mute the horror of combat on civilians, and to create the basis for diplomatic settlement.[22]

The proliferation of organisations working in conflict prevention and resolution and the increasingly vocal demands for bans or restrictions on the arms trade, landmines and the exploitation of children are indications of a paradigm shift in global affairs. As the degree of co-operation between states, IGOs and non-state actors increases, the degree of accountability and responsibility for all sides will also increase. The aim is to ensure that waging war becomes a less attractive option than peaceful negotiations.

Conclusion

In the Introduction to this book we asked why it was that the conflicts such as those in Bosnia and Rwanda were not prevented. We questioned the capacity of existing international organisations and structures to tackle the range of internal conflicts that have become prevalent in recent years. We suggested that the time had come for a new framework for tackling such conflicts to allow for the transformation of violent conflict into peaceful disputes. In creating this new framework, we highlighted the need for greater collaboration between state organs and the wealth of non-state organisations that have emerged.

Conflict transformation as discussed in this book is not just about the short-term conflict prevention or resolution of ongoing wars. Rather, it is a fundamental conceptual shift in the way global security issues are addressed. It is rooted in the belief that, first, those who are directly affected by conflict must participate in peacemaking process; second, it champions the growth and development of an *international civil society*, where a network of state, non-state and community movements complement each other's actions in creating and sustaining peace; and third, it argues that if peaceful negotiations are made more attractive than waging war, there is a great chance that the practice of warfare in general will decline throughout the world.

Within this new paradigm, the notion of global and national security, previously defined in terms of global superstructures, military technology and defence policies governed by set attitudes and perception, is being redefined in terms of *people's security*. Nuclear proliferation is still a major concern, but now environmental degradation, poverty and illness, extreme nationalism and social fragmentation also threaten our collective sense of human security. In other words, if people are not living in peace, if they are marginalised or face oppression or violence, and their security is threatened, then increasingly the state itself is threatened Our collective global security is no longer in the domain of superpower relations.

Increasingly, it is dependent on the individual and collective relationships of people within communities and within states.

Those who currently have responsibility for global security issues, namely the UN Security Council, the Secretary General, General Assembly, and governments world-wide, are gradually taking these factors into account and altering their practices accordingly. The EU and the OAU are taking very concrete steps towards redefining their mandates in relation to conflict prevention. The governments of Japan, the Scandanavian countries and others are revisiting their development aid policies and building coherence into their defence aid and trade policies. In the final analysis it is a question of a profound shift in political will and choice: the will to reassess their priorities and concerns within a global context; and the choice to divert some percentage of 'defence' and 'security' expenditure away from the military and into non-military routes.

No doubt the practice of multi-track diplomacy and burden-sharing will face significant challenges in the years to come. A great deal of work still needs to be done on their theoretical and practical implications. The efficacy of involving business and industry, the media and other social sectors into this framework is still being worked on. As indicated previously, there is a need to establish mutual accountability, responsibility and an agreed code of conduct or guidelines for intervention and mediation into intra-state conflicts between states, IGOs and NGOs. Yet, despite these current shortcomings, the debate continues. New initiatives and ideas are gaining ground. The prevention of violent conflict and the elimination of warfare are becoming a concrete possibility for the future of humanity.

Notes

Introduction

1. Peter Maas, *Love Thy Neighbour – A Story of War* (London: Papermac, 1996), p. 273.
2. Though the Holocaust is a term used in reference to the genocide of six million Jews, it is important to note that millions of Poles, Russians, Gypsies and other people were also victims of systematic slaughter.
3. Maas, *Love thy Neighbour*, p. 116.
4. Alex Schmid and A.J. Jongman, *Mapping Violent Conflicts and Human Rights Violations in the mid-1990s*, (Leiden: PIOOM, 1997).
5. Schmid and Jongman, *Mapping Violent Conflicts*.
6. A notable exception is Sri Lanka where civilian casualties account for approximately 50 per cent of the total. John F. Burns, 'Bomb's Fallout Adds to the Gloom Hanging over Sri Lanka', *The New York Times*, 17 October 1997, p. A7.
7. The discussion presented here is based on the work of Adam Curle discussed in John Paul Lederach, *Preparing for Peace Conflict Transformation Across Cultures* (Syracuse: Syracuse University Press, 1995), pp. 12–15.

Chapter 1

1. Quoted in Sattareh Farman-Farmaian and Dona Munker, *Daughter of Persia* (New York: Archer Books, 1993), p. 26.
2. Mahmood Mamdani, *Citizen and Subject – Contemporary Africa and the Legacy of Late Colonialism* (London: James Currey, 1996).
3. Samuel Huntington, 'The Clash of Civilisations', *Foreign Affairs*, Vol. 72, No. 3 (Summer 1993).
4. Thomas Homer-Dixon and V. Percival, *Environmental Scarcity and Violent Conflict: The Case of Rwanda*. Occasional Paper, Project on Environment, Population and Security. Peace & Conflict Studies, University of Toronto, June 1995.
5. Kevin Watkins, *Oxfam Poverty Report* (Oxford: Oxfam Publications, 1995), p. 4.
6. Watkins, *Oxfam*, p. 4.
7. Watkins, *Oxfam*, p. 78.
8. Schmid and Jongman, *Mapping Violent Conflicts*.
9. The recent international agreement to ban landmines is a significant and positive development, but de-mining existing areas will still take years.

10. The Conservative governments of Mrs Thatcher and Mr Major were accused of supporting the sale of equipment to Iraq which could have been used for weapons development, despite policies which forbade such trade.

11. Despite the UN Security Council order that Iraq surrender or destroy its germ warfare capabilities after the Gulf War in 1991, Saddam Hussein's government has successfully evaded the UN's special investigative commission. A.M. Rosenthal, 'The Chosen Weapon', *The New York Times*, 17 October 1997, p. A35.

12. Of the 100 major conflicts that took place between 1945 and 1990, leaving an estimated 20 million people dead, the United Nations was powerless to act in most of them. With either American, Chinese or Russian interests at stake, the Security Council regularly vetoed any calls for UN intervention. The original Security Council members were the United States, Great Britain, formerly the Soviet Union (now Russia), France, and in the 1970s, China. Council members have the right to veto any decisions or actions proposed by the General Assembly of the UN. Only on Korea was UN intervention agreed and that was due to the Soviets boycotting the vote.

13. Boutros Boutros-Ghali, *An Agenda for Peace* (New York: United Nations, 1992).

14. Chapter IV of the UN Charter relates to the Pacific Settlement of Disputes.

15. UN Charter, Chapter I Purposes & Principles.

16. Chapter VII, Articles 41 and 42 of the Charter state that the Security Council can call upon the use of all measures (including land, air and sea forces) to maintain or restore international peace and security.

17. Boutros Boutros-Ghali, *Supplement to an Agenda for Peace* (New York: United Nations, 1995).

18. Stanley Hoffman, 'On the Ethics of Intervention' 'Letter to the Editor', *Survival*, Spring 1996, p. 181.

19. Louise Diamond and John McDonald, *Multi-track Diplomacy: A Systems Approach to Peace* (3rd edition), (Washington, D.C.: Kumarian Press, 1993)

20. These data are taken from Schmid and Jongman, *Mapping Violent Conflicts*.

Chapter 2

1. Carolyn Nordstrom, *The Dirty War: Civilian Experiences of Conflict in Mozambique and Sri Lanka* in K. Rupesinghe (ed.), Internal Conflict and Governance (London: Macmillan, 1992), pp. 27–43.

2. Data for 1996 obtained from *PIOOM/FEWER World Conflict Map 1996* (Leiden: PIOOM, 1997).

3. The second IRA ceasefire was announced on 19 July 1997. At the time of writing, this ceasefire had just been announced.

4. Martin Van Creveld, *Future War* (New York: Free Press, 1991).

5. P.Calvocoressi p. 14.

6. These definitions are also used by the PIOOM, and are generally accepted amongst international war and conflict researchers.

7. Alex Schmid and A.J Jongman, *Mapping Violent Conflicts and Human Rights Violations in the mid-1990s*. PIOOM Newsletter and Progress Report (Leiden: PIOOM, 1997).

8. Ted Robert Gurr, 'Minorities Report (1) Ethnopolitical Conflicts in the 1990s: Patterns and Trends', available at URL, www.bsos.umd.edu/cidcm/mar/minrept1.htm (1997).

9. In the case of Central Africa, this has proved to be true. At the time of writing, widespread violence and conflict were being reported in the Republic of Congo, with the involvement of Angola. Also in that region, Uganda and Rwanda were reportedly highly influential in their support for Laurent Kabila and the eventual downfall of President Mobuto Sese Seko. Howard French, 'Africa Finds Old Borders Are Eroding', *The New York Times*, 18 October 1997, pp. A1, A7.

10. SIPRI 1996 report

11. From the works of Johan Galtung, quoted in Felipe. E. MacGregor, S.J. and Marcial Rubio C., 'Rejoinder to the Theory of Structural Violence', in Kumar Rupesinghe and C. Marcial Rubio, *The Culture of Violence* (Tokyo: United Nations University Press, 1994), pp. 42–55.

12. Adapted from NGO Networking Service and InterAfrica Group, *Demobilisation and Reintegration – Issues in the Horn of Africa*, Issues Notes, No. 2, p. 5.

13. William Zartman (ed.), *Elusive Peace* (Washington, D.C.: The Brookings Institution, 1995), pp. 3–17, 332–45 (here and below).

14. Zartman, *Elusive Peace*.

15. *Guardian*, 8 August 1996.

16. Wayne E. Nafziger, 'The Economics of Humanitarian Emergencies: From Bosnia to Rwanda' (UNU/WIDER), January 1997.

17. Nafziger, 'Humanitarian Emergencies'.

18. Thomas Homer-Dixon, 'Environmental Scarcity and Violent Conflict: The Case of Rwanda', *Occasional Paper for the Project on Environment, Population and Security*, Peace & Conflict Studies (Canada: University of Toronto), June 1995.

19. Robin Clarke, *Water: The International Crisis* (London: Earthscan Publications Ltd, 1991).

20. Homer-Dixon, 'Environmental Scarcity and Violent Conflict: The Case of Gaza' *Occasional Paper for the Project on Environment, Population and Security*. Peace & Conflict Studies (Canada: University of Toronto), June 1995.

21. Raimo Väyrynen, 'Political Causes of Humanitarian Emergencies: State Failure and Protracted Crises', draft paper presented at the UNU/WIDER-Queen Elizabeth House Meeting on the Political Economy of the Prevention of Humanitarian Emergencies (Oxford University, 3–5 July 1997).

22. Väyrynen, 'Political Causes of Humanitarian Emergencies'.

23. The US government was directly involved in the overthrow of Prime Minister Mohammad Mossadeq in Iran in 1953 and of President Salvador Allende in Chile in 1973. In its tacit support for South Africa's destabilisation policy in Angola and Mozambique, the US was also partly responsible for the escalation of war in both countries throughout the 1980s.

24. International Institute of Strategic Studies, *Strategic Survey* (Oxford: Oxford University Press, 1996).
25. Benedict Anderson, *Imagined Communities* (London:Verso, 1993).
26. Frank Abate (gen. project ed.), *The Oxford Dictionary and Thesaurus, American Edition* (New York: Oxford University Press, 1996), p. 727.
27. See Francis Fukuyama, *The End of History and the Last Man* (London: Hamilton, 1992), p. xiii.
28. For more on the future of politics, see Anthony Giddens, *Beyond Left and Right: The Future of Radical Politics* (Cambridge: Polity Press, 1994).
29. 'Armed and Dangerous', *Guardian G2*, 18 May 1995, p. 7.
30. It is worth noting here that the overlap between ideology, ethnicity and religion re-emphasise the fluid nature of any typology of internal conflicts.
31. Edward Azar, 'Management of Protracted Social Conflict in the Third World', paper prepared for the Fourth ICES Annual Lecture at Columbia University (unpublished), New York, 10 June 1986.
32. Azar, Protracted Social Conflict.
33. Adapted from Björn Hettne, 'Models of Ethnic Stratification', *Etniske Konflikter og internationella relationer*.
34. At the time of writing new efforts were being made to resume substantive talks between the two sides.
35. The Muslims did fight back, but the Serbs were always better equipped and had control of the Yugoslav national army at the time of the state's break-up.
36. With reference to Anthony Smith, 'Towards a Theory of Separatism', in *Ethnic and Racial Studies*, Vol. 2, No. 1 (1979).
37. It is worth noting that over 2,000 years ago Roman soldiers were not paid regular salaries either. Their survival depended on conquering and looting territories, but their rights to various goods and valuables were determined according to strict rank and hierarchy.
38. Alex de Waal, 'War and Rural Development in Africa', *IDS Bulletin*, Vol. 27, No. 3 (1996).
39. de Waal, 'War and Rural Development'.
40. de Waal, 'War and Rural Development'.
41. 'Behind the White Lines', *Sunday Times Magazine*, 22 February 1997, pp. 27–33.
42. Michael Sheridan Vientiane, 'Heroin Chiefs Hit Ho Chi Minh Trail', *Sunday Times*, 3 November 1996, p. 24.
43. Jonathan Freedland, 'Guns, Plots and Warlike Poses', *Guardian*, 6 May 1995, p. 25.
44. Azar, Protracted Social Conflict.

Chapter 3

1. Reprinted in the *Independent on Sunday*, 31 January 1993.
2. Adapted from Sharon Rusu, 'The Role of ReliefWeb', in Susanne Schmeidl and Howard Adelman, *Synergy in Early Warning; Conference Proceedings* (Toronto: Centre for International and Security Studies, Forum on Early Warning and Early Response, 1997), p. 255.

3. This section and Figure 3.1 are an adaptation of a typology of conflict escalation by Alex Schmid and A.J. Jongman, 'Mapping Violent Conflicts and Human Rights in the mid-1990s' (Leiden: PIOOM 1997), and of 'The Continuum from Harmony to War – A Barometer of Peace and Conflict', in Michael Lund, *Preventing and Mitigating Violent Conflicts: A Guide to Practitioners* (Washington, D.C.: Creative Associates International Inc., 1996), pp. 5–8.

4. Harmony exists within different groups, and arguably a harmony of sorts is evident when an entire nation is at war with an external enemy, but under normal conditions there are always some social tensions.

5. Michael Lund, 'When Dogs of War Don't Bark: Explaining Peaceful Settlement of Ethnic Kin-Group Conflicts Between Emerging Post-Communist States', unpublished draft manuscript, June 1997.

6. Of course, within months the entire country had been taken over.

7. Londoners are made aware of the conflict through sporadic bombing campaigns and by virtue of living in a city where basic amenities such as public rubbish bins in transport depots have been removed for fear of bombs.

8. With acknowledgements to Lund, *Preventing and Mitigating Violent Conflicts*, pp. 3–11.

9. Lund, *Preventing and Mitigating Violent Conflicts*, pp. 3–12.

10. The collapse of the pyramid savings schemes in early 1997, which have effectively wiped out the savings of thousands of people, and the government's inept response, has, at the time of writing, led to violence and political crisis.

11. Lund, *Preventing and Mitigating Violent Conflict*, pp. 3–8.

12. ReliefWeb available at http://www.reliefweb.int.

13. Rusu, 'The Role of ReliefWeb', pp. 257–8.

14. J.G. Siccama (ed.), *Conflict Prevention and Early Warning in the Political Practice of International Organisations* (The Netherlands: Clingendael Institute, 1996).

15. For more information on the World Bank's programme on post-conflict reconstruction refer to *A Framework for World Bank Involvement in Post-Conflict Reconstruction* (Washington, D.C: World Bank Publications, 1997).

16. For details of ongoing research projects refer to Jane Holl, *Carnegie Commission on Preventing Deadly Conflict, Second Progress Report* (New York: Carnegie Corporation of New York, July 1996).

17. The Minorities at Risk Project, State Failures Project, UN HEWS & HCR, World Vision, and Barbara Harff's conflict triggers and accelerators are examples of some of the ongoing work in this area.

18. Adapted from Ted Gurr's *State Failures Project* set of indicators.

19. Joint Evaluation of Emergency Assistance to Rwanda, *The International Response to Conflict and Genocide: Lessons from the Rwanda Experience. Synthesis Report*, March 1996.

20. Margaret Buchanan-Smith and Susanna Davies, *Famine Early Warning and Response – The Missing Link* (London: Intermediate Technologies Publications, 1995), pp. 204–11.

21. Jacqueline Damon, *Conflict Prevention and Co-ordination in the Field of Development Co-operation, OECD Report* (Berlin: OECD, 1996).
22. John G. Cockell, 'Towards Response-Orientated Early Warning Analysis: Policy and Operational Considerations', *Synergy in Early Warning – Conference Proceedings March 15–18 1997* (Toronto: Centre for International and Security Studies York University), pp. 289–96.
23. International Alert heads the FEWER Secretariat.
24. With reference to Donald G. McNeil, 'The Dead Zone', *The New York Times*, 27 May 1997, and Donald G. McNeil, 'In Congo, Forbidding Terrain Hides a Calamity', *The New York Times*, 1 June 1997.
25. McNeil, 'In Congo'.
26. Many of the 'tools' mentioned here are adapted from Michael Lund, *Preventing and Mitigating Violent Conflicts: An Abridged Practitioner's Guide* (Washington, D.C.: Creative Associates International Inc., 1997), pp. 19–24.
27. The figure comes from Michael Lund, *Preventing and Mitigating Violent Conflicts: A Guide for Practitioners* (Washington, D.C.: Creative Associates International Inc., 1996), pp. 3–18.
28. With thanks to Michael Lund, *Preventing and Mitigating Violent Conflict*, pp. 4–6.
29. The arguments put forward in this section have been adapted from Kalypo Nicolaidis' paper, 'International Preventive Action; Developing a Strategic Framework', in Robert Rotberg (ed.), *Vigilance and Vengeance, NGOs Preventing Ethnic Conflicts in Divided Societies* (Washington, D.C.: The Brookings Institution/WPF, 1996) pp. 23–69.

Chapter 4

1. Quoted in Tran Van Dinh, *Communication and Diplomacy in a Changing World* (New Jersey: Ablex Publishing Corporation, 1987), p. 3.
2. Tran Van Dinh *Communication*, p. 2.
3. Mentioned in Keith Hamilton and Richard Langhorne, *The Practice of Diplomacy* (London: Routledge, 1995), pp. 3–7.
4. Ilya Gershevitch (ed.), *Cambridge History of Iran Book 2: The Median and Achaemenian Periods* (Cambridge: Cambridge University Press, 1985), pp. 315–16.
5. *The American Heritage Dictionary of the English Language, New College Edition* (Boston: Houghton Mifflin Company, 1976).
6. Much of the discussion in this section is attributed to Hamilton and Langhorne, *Practice of Diplomacy* (1995).
7. George Podiebard, *King of Bohemia*, quoted in M. Anderson, *The Rise of Modern Diplomacy 1450–1990* (London: Longman, 1993), p. 210.
8. Emeric Crucé, 'Le Nouveau Cynée, ou Discours d'Estat representant les Occasions et Moyens d'establir une Paix générale et la Liberté du Commerce par tout Le Monde' (Paris 1623), quoted in Anderson, *Modern Diplomacy*, p. 216.

9. Quoted in Harold Nicolson, *The Evolution of Diplomatic Method* (London: Constable, 1954), p. 87.

10. In the early years China was represented by a delegation from the Nationalist government of Taiwan. This changed in 1971 when the General Assembly voted to seat a delegation from the People's Republic of China instead.

11. United Nations, *Handbook on the Peaceful Settlement of Disputes between States* (New York: United Nations, 1992), p. 155.

12. By 1960 the USA, Canada and Japan had joined, changing the name to the Organisation for Economic Co-operation and Development (OECD), and expanding its activities to a number of developing countries. In 1994 it was expanded and renamed once again as the OSCE, the Organisation for Security and Co-operation in Europe.

13. Article 71 (Chapter X) of the UN Charter states 'The Economic and Social Council may make any suitable arrangement for consultation with non-governmental organisations which are concerned with matters within its competence.'

14. For detailed information please refer to United Nations, *Handbook on the Peaceful Settlement of Disputes between States* (New York: United Nations, 1992).

15. Refer to Article 7 (Chapter I) and Articles 39–42 (Chapter VII) of the UN Charter.

16. Boutros Boutros-Ghali, *Agenda for Peace* (New York: United Nations, 1992)

17. 'Declaration on the Rules of International Humanitarian Law Governing the Conduct of Hostilities in Non-international Armed Conflict', extract from *the International Review of the Red Cross,* September–October 1990, No. 278, pp. 404–8.

18. NGO figures drawn from Michael Edwards and David Hulme, *Non-Governmental Organisations – Performance and Accountability* (London: Earthscan, 1996), pp. 3–5.

19. Many people regard eating healthily and taking exercise as a form of prevention against future illnesses.

20. At the time of writing two Hamas suicide bombers had detonated two bombs in a Jerusalem market. The talks which were on the verge of commencing were stalled again.

21. Alternatively it has been described as a 'web of interconnected parts (activities, individuals, institutions, communities) that operate together, whether awkwardly or gracefully, for a common goal: a world at peace'. Louise Diamond and John McDonald, *Multi-track Diplomacy: A Systems Approach to Peace*, 3rd edition (Washington, D.C.: Kumarian Press, 1996).

22. Joseph V Montville, *Conflict and Peace in Multi-Ethnic Societies* (Lexington, Mass: Lexington Books, 1991), p. 162.

23. Michael Cassidy, *A Witness Forever* (London: Hodder & Stoughton, 1995).

24. Adapted from *Newsweek Magazine*, 20 October 1997.

25. In Rwanda certain elements within the church were involved in the genocide.

26. Cameron Hume, *Ending Mozambique's War* (Washington: United States Institute of Peace, 1994).

27. Cynthia Sampson, 'Quaker Conciliation during the Nigerian Civil War', in D. Johnstone and C. Sampson (eds.), *Religion: the Missing Dimension in Statecraft* (Oxford: Oxford University Press, 1993).

28. D. Johnstone and C. Sampson, *Religion* (Oxford: Oxford University Press 1993), Chapter 5.

29. Edmundo Garcia, personal discussions.

30. *The European Union and the Issue of Conflict Prevention in Africa: Peace-building, Conflict Prevention and Beyond* SEC(96) 332, Communication from the European Commission to the Council on Peace Building, March 1996.

31. The triangle is adapted from Jean Paul Lederach's 'Actors and Peace Building Foci Across the Affected Populations'.

32. 'Israel's Serial Bungler', in *The Economist*, 11 October 1997, pp. 17, 49.

33. These are just a few examples from a list of over 400 projects published in the *Northern Ireland Community Relations Council Sixth Annual Report 1996* (Belfast: Northern Ireland Community Relations Council), pp. 23–31.

34. Institute for Resources and Security Studies, Preventing Deadly Intergroup Conflict, A Guide for the Preparation of Evidence, Version 1.0 (Cambridge, Mass: IRSS, 1996), pp. 15–18.

Chapter 5

1. Quoted in the UN war-torn societies project web site at http://www.unrisd.org/voice.htm.

2. The latest accord has held, and democratic elections were planned for May 1997, but previously an estimated 14 accords were broken.

3. The Dayton Accord has not been broken, but nor is it being upheld fully in terms of the measures that each side was to take within the given timetable. Furthermore, reports from Mostar indicate that Croat factions have been persecuting Muslims once again.

4. These figures are drawn from the works of Paul Pillar and Roy Licklider as cited in Charles King, *Ending Civil Wars* (Adelphi Paper 308, Oxford University Press, 1997), pp. 24–5.

5. King, *Ending Civil Wars*, p. 27.

6. International Alert, 'Tools for Conflict Transformation' list, adapted from Dereck Denniston, *Defending the Land with Maps* (London: World Watch, Jan/Feb. 1994).

7. King, *Ending Civil Wars*, p. 73.

8. Adapted from ACORD, *EC Rehabilitation Project in Eritrea: Project of Returnees and De-mobilised 'Fighters' in Nine Settlements in Four Provinces, Report* (London; ACORD, June 1996).

9. E.J. Laurance and S. Meek, *The New Field of Micro-Disarmament: Addressing the Proliferation and Build-up of Small Arms & Light Weapons* (Bonn: Bonn International Centre for Conversion, September 1996), Brief 7, Appendix 8.

10. J. Pearce, 'Impunity and Democracy; the Case of Chile', in Rachel Sieder (ed.), *Impunity in Latin America* (London: Institute of Latin American Studies, 1995), pp. 45–54.
11. Adapted from the Centre for the Independence of Judges and Lawyers (CIJL) Yearbook, *The Judiciary in Transition* (Dijon: CIJL, 1994).
12. Earthaction, 'An International Criminal Court, Editorial Advisory' (London: Earthaction, June 1997).
13. According to Amnesty International the term 'crimes against humanity' should encompass a wide range of acts including widespread and systematic murder, extermination of a group, forced disappearances of persons, torture, rape, prostitution and other sexual abuses, arbitrary deportation and forcible transfer of populations, arbitrary imprisonment and enslavement. 'Basic Definitions Regarding the ICC', Amnesty International Index: IOR 40/01/97; January 1997.
14. Amnesty International, 'Basic Definitions'.
15. Kofi Annan, quoted in *Canadian Network for an International Criminal Court*.
16. Barnen och Vi, *Swedish Save the Children*, Report No. 2/88.
17. Graca Machal, 'Impact of Armed Conflict on Children', UN General Assembly A/51/306, August 1996.
18. Machal, 'Impact of Armed Conflict'.
19. 'Declaration on the Rules of International Humanitarian Law Governing the Conduct of Hostilities in Non-international Armed Conflict', Extract from *the International Review of the Red Cross*, September–October 1990, No. 278, pp. 404–8.
20. Ernest Gellner, *Conditions of Liberty, Civil Society and its Rivals* (London: Penguin, 1996).
21. The Hague Appeal for Peace, *Initial Announcement* for the 'Civil Society's Campaign Conference', November 1997.
22. Nicholas O. Berry, *War and the Red Cross: The Unspoken Mission* (London: Macmillan, 1997), pp. 30–1.

Select Bibliography

Adelman, H. and S. Schmeidl (eds), *Synergy in Early Warning*, Conference Proceedings, Toronto: Centre for International and Security Studies, Forum for Early Warning and Early Response, March 1997.

Alker, H. et al. (eds), Conflict Early Warnings System (CEWS) working papers series, presented at the (CEWS) Steering Committee Meeting, London: International Alert, 19–21 June 1996.

Berry, Nicholas O., *War and the Red Cross: The Unspoken Mission*, London: Macmillan, 1997.

Boutros-Ghali, B., *An Agenda for Peace*, New York: United Nations, 1992.

Buchanon-Smith, M. and S. Davies, *Famine Early Warning and Response – The Missing Link*, London: Intermediate Technology Publications, 1995.

Diamond, L. and J. McDonald, *Multi-Track Diplomacy: A Systems Approach to Peace* (3rd edition), Washington, D.C.: Kumarian Press, 1993.

Doucet, I. (ed.), *Resource Pack for Conflict Transformation*, London: International Alert, 1996.

Holl, J., *Carnegie Commission on Preventing Deadly Conflict, Second Progress Report*, New York: Carnegie Corporation of New York, 1996.

Homer-Dixon, T. and V. Percival (eds), *Occasional Papers, Project on Environment, Population and Security*, Toronto: Peace & Conflict Studies, University of Toronto, June 1995.

King, C., *Ending Civil Wars*, Adelphi Paper 308, Oxford: Oxford University Press, 1997.

Kuroda, M. and K. Rupesinghe (eds), *Early Warning and Conflict Resolution*, London: Macmillan, 1992.

Lederach, J.P., *Preparing for Peace, Conflict Transformation Across Cultures*, Syracuse: Syracuse University Press, 1995.

Lund, M., *Preventing and Mitigating Violent Conflict: A Guide for Practitioners*, Washington, D.C.: Creative Associates International Inc., 1996.

Maas, P., *Love Thy Neighbour – A Story of War*, London: Papermac, 1996.

Mamdani, M., *Citizen and Subject, Contemporary Africa and the Legacy of Late Colonialism*, London: James Currey, 1996.

Rupesinghe, K., 'From Civil War to Civil Peace: Multi-track Solutions to Armed Conflict', *Multilateralism and the UN System*, UNU Symposium, Costa Rica, 18–19 December 1995.

Rupesinghe, K., (ed.), *Conflict Transformation*, Basingstoke: Macmillan, 1995.

Rupesinghe, K. and Marcial Rubio, C., *The Culture of Violence*, Tokyo: United Nations University, 1994.

Naftziger, W. et al. (eds), *War, Hunger and Destitution: The Political Economy of the Prevention of Humanitarian Emergencies*, Volumes I–III, UNU/WIDER, 1998.

167

de Waal, A., 'War and Rural Development in Africa', *IDS Bulletin*, Vol. 27, No. 3, 1996.

Watkin, K., *Oxfam Poverty Report*, Oxford: Oxfam Publications, 1995.

Zartman, W., (ed.), *Elusive Peace*, Washington, D.C.: The Brookings Institution, 1995.

Index

Index by Auriol Griffith-Jones